LAKELAND VILLAGE
ADAPTIVE
BEHAVIOR
GRID
MANUAL

By
GRANT O. GILBERT, PhD
TERRY L. MADSEN, MS

PUBLISHED BY

Copyright © 1985
By

TristanGilbert.com
PO Box 96
Twisp, WA 98856

First Experimental Version..1973
Experimental Version Revised..1976
Experimental Version Revised..1978
First Published Edition 1985
Library of Congress Catalog Number: 84-090595
International Standard Book Number: 0-9613632-0-7
Second Published Edition..2008

International Standard Book Number: 978-0-6152-1184-8

Contents

Acknowledgements

Many people have contributed to the development of the Lakeland Village Adaptive Behavior Grid. First, the authors thank Dr. G. Newton Buker, former superintendant at Lakeland Village and Dr. Jack Bratten, former director of the psychology department. Without their encouragement and support, the Grid would not exist today.

Next, all of the members of Lakeland's psychology department are acknowledged for their generous cooperation and excellent ideas. These people contributed many hours of assistance, especially in item selection and field testing. Especially helpful was the standardization data collected by Mark Smedley, one of the department members. He deserves special thanks and recognition for this effort.

Finally, the authors extend their appreciation to Lakeland Village's attendant counselors for their devotion to and accurate knowledge of Lakeland's residents. These people have patiently served as informants for thousands of Grid assessments.

To acknowledge each contributor to the Grid is not possible. However, a number of people are of special significance in the Grid's development. These people are listed below:

Jerry Anderson	Kathy Kipp
Mary Branting	Sue Lehinger
Cliff Christiansen	Judy Murphy
Ruth Highness	Gwen Nichols
Al Kertes	Nancy Sexton

Introduction

A number of psychological instruments enjoy a well-deserved reputation for their capacity to measure the severity or degree of retarded mental functioning. For approximately three-quarters of a century, such tests have been used to group clients for care and treatment. Among the most common instruments are the Stanford-Binet Intelligence Scale invented in its original form for just this purpose and several scales more recently developed by David Wechsler.

For more than a decade, there has been general dissatisfaction with the exclusive use of intelligence tests to define mental retardation. The American Association on Mental Deficiency (AAMD) has taken a position in this respect and requires evidence of deficiency in adaptive behavior as well as in intellectual functioning (measured intelligence) before an individual is to be classified as mentally retarded.

There is a lack of universal agreement as to the meaning of adaptive behavior; although, in gereral, it is viewed as applied intelligence. Perhaps the notion that is most useful to workers in the field of mental retardation is found in the AAMD manual on classification in mental retardation (Grossman, 1983) where adaptive behavior is defined as, "the effectiveness or degree with which individuals meet the standards of personal independence and social responsibility expected for age and cultural group." Conversely, the AAMD manual defines impairments in adaptive behavior "as significant limitations in an individual's effectiveness in meeting the standards of maturation, learning, personal independence, and/or social responsibility that are expected for his or her age level and cultural group, as determined by clinical assessment and, usually, standardized tests."

There have been numerous attempts to objectively assess adaptive behavior. One survey of behavior checklists (Cone & Hawkins, 1976) located more than 250 checklists, many specifically addressed to the assessment of adaptive behavior skills in special populations such as mentally retarded persons. Some of the checklists have items known to represent the average or typical performance for persons of specific age levels. This information enables users to compare a client with "...standards of personal independence and social responsibility expected of his age...". Other checklists utilize items which the list constructors arbitrarily selected as standards; sometimes with, and other times without the aid of other "expert opinion." Still other checklists are standardized on populations of mentally retarded persons and enable comparisons with that population.

The *Lakeland Village Adaptive Behavior Grid* is a checklist of the first type described above. The items are age-valued, thus enabling a user to compare a client with standards of adaptive behavior found in the community. The *Grid*, as it has come to be called by its users, has its roots in the 1973 revision of the AAMD classification manual. This manual contains a table of many adaptive behavior examples organized into ten skill categories: independent functioning, (eating, toileting, dressing, and cleanliness), physical, communication, social, economic activity, occupation, and self-direction. One of the authors of the Grid analyzed this table and found that the levels of development therein described, roughly resemble nine levels of normal development: 6 months, 1 year, 2 years, 3 years, 4 years, 5 years, 8 years, 12 years, and 16 years.

The short descriptive statements in the AAMD table served as a nucleus for developing the Grid. The authors scoured the developmental literature as well as other checklists in search of age-valued performance statements similar in content to the AAMD adaptive behavior statements. Many such statements were found and organized into a huge matrix or "Grid" with skill category defining one dimension and age level defining the other.

Numerous sources provided the behavior statements that appear in the Grid. The primary reference was the Gesell Institute Behavior Profiles contained in several books spanning the development of children from birth through maturity. Other references which served mainly as corroborative evidence for the age placement of items were the *Vineland Social Maturity Scale*, the *Bayley Scales of Infant Development*, the *Merrill-Palmer Scale of Mental Tests*, the *Stanford-Binet Intelligence Test*, the *Wide Range Achievement Test*, the *Denver Developmental Screening Test*, the *Developmental Profile*, and the two child development books by Caplan (1980). In addition, a number of checklists were collected, studied, and used for guidance to insure that no important skills were overlooked. Among these checklists were the *Behavioral Characteristics Progression Charts*, the *Washington Assessment & Training Scales*, the *Nebraska Client Progress System*, the *AAMD Adaptive Behavior Scale*, the *Developmental Record*, and the *Koontz Child Developmental Program*.

In the process of organizing the Grid, the original AAMD table of adaptive behavior illustrations was modified. The content of the skill categories, economic activity and self-direction, appeared to overlap with communication and occupation; so the four were combined into two and labeled Communication and Vocation & Recreation. Two new skill categories, Orientation and Behavior Control (later changed to Self-Direction) were added; and several of the original category names were changed. Moreover, because a large portion of the Lakeland Village population was profoundly mentally retarded, 3 month and 18 month levels were added to increase coverage at the extreme lower developmental range.

The present Grid consists of ten skill clusters: Eating, Toileting, Dressing, Health & Grooming, Communication, Mobility & Dexterity, Vocation & Recreation, Socialization, Orientation, and Self-Direction. Skills are described for eleven developmental levels: 3 months, 6 months, 12 months, 18 months, 2 years, 3 years, 4 years, 5 years, 8 years, 12 years, and 16 years. Each cell in the Grid—skill cluster by developmental level—contains five separate descriptions of behavior. Each description is viewed as one instance of the general skill. Satisfactory performance of the five behaviors is regarded as evidence that the client has mastered the skill cluster at that level; less than total success is viewed as partial mastery.

Early in the Grid's use at Lakeland Village, the usual method for completing an asessment was for a psychologist to collect information about a client's capabilities by interviewing attendants, teachers, parents, etc. Interviews were supplemented by actually testing the performance on Grid items that were readily amenable to testing. For example, attendants were asked to say whether or not a client "practices social conventions without prompting (i.e., expresses appropriate greetings and farewells)" and the judgement of the informant was used as a basis for giving credit or not giving credit in the skill (Socialization at the 8 year level). On the other hand, whether or not a client can "alternate feet going down stairs" was usually determined by requesting a demonstration of that skill (Mobility & Dexterity at the 4 year level).

After Lakeland's staff became familiar with the Grid and the Grid items, then assessment became somewhat streamlined. Instruction in conducting Grid assessments became a formal part of Lakeland's staff development program. Most Grid assessments at Lakeland are now conducted without the interview process by the psychologist. Persons in each of several disciplines (including direct-service personnel) independently complete those portions or items with which they are familiar. The psychologist compiles the input, adds his or her input, checks the items for obvious errors or discrepancies, and then performs the final scoring. Staff are instructed not to guess on questionable items, but rather to leave questionable items blank until they are tested (preferably right away). Persons conducting Grid assesments are given the option of (1) completing a Grid from the beginning with a blank Assessment Record, or (2) taking the most recent Grid assessment for that client and updating it by adding and deleting items credited. This latter method is more efficient since fewer items need to evaluated due to the savings from one assessment to the next. In addition, the first method tends to encourage guessing because of the time factor in testing items which may already have been tested.

At the present time, the Grid exists in two forms. An extended version is contained in the Skill Cluster Descriptions, while an abbreviated version is used to conduct the actual client assessment. The latter version, called the Assessment Record, consists of brief one-line statements followed by a space for recording the client's successful performance of the behavior. Usually, the brief statement is incomplete by itself, and the Skill Cluster Descriptions must be consulted for a better understanding of the behavior being assessed. An assessment yields a developmental level score for each of the ten skill clusters, a composite score called the average developmental level (ADL), and an indication of which items the client does and does not perform.

The Grid has many applications. One principal use is the determination of a client's training needs. For example, the matrix-like structure enables the user to graphically compare a client's strengths and weaknesses across the ten skill clusters. This information is then useful for suggesting specific areas and items needing special attention. Also, the Grid—being hierarchical in structure—is helpful in revealing gaps in a client's repertoire of skills. It is widely recognized that complex skills are built upon preceding skills that must be learned in a stepwise fashion. When all of the earlier steps are not mastered, further learning is impaired. Once revealed, however, these gaps in learning can be filled in and further progress expedited.

Another principal application of the Grid is the classification of the adaptive behavior of clients. At this time, there are no generally accepted procedures for using the information from adaptive behavior assessments to classify the adaptive behavior of mentally retarded persons. The Grid manual describes an objective procedure for arriving at an adaptive behavior classification given a client's chronological age and the composite score from the Grid. The procedure is reliable, has demonstrated validity, and allows for adjustments based upon clinical judgement of the situation.

Since its conception in 1973, the Grid has undergone several revisions. In this 1984 revision, all of the Skill Cluster Descriptions have been rewritten, primarily for the purpose of further clarification. Also, a small number of items have been changed because of problems that have been noted during use. Several items have been added. The Grid has been in use at Lakeland Village since late 1973. Informally, it has been shared with over 400 interested professionals throughout the country. A number of these persons have reported that they are employing the Grid in their respective programs.

In conclusion, the *Lakeland Village Adaptive Behavior Grid* is a behavior checklist specifically designed for assessing the skills, training needs, and progress of mentally retarded clients. The Grid is probably also useful in a wider context since its major content was derived from descriptions of the general population. The performance items carry a value which is the approximate age level when the skill is usually mastered; therefore, the Grid can be distinguished from many other similar tools. This feature enables the user to compare a client's performance with standards that reflect the expected performance of people in the community. The Grid has undergone several revisions since it was first conceived in 1973. It has been in use at Lakeland Village since late 1973.

Administering and Scoring

Grid assessments should only be conducted by persons with demonstrated understanding of the steps involved. The assessment process involves recording (including judgements regarding whether credit is given or not given for specific items), providing information about the skills of clients (informant), the testing of questionable items, and scoring. One or more persons may be involved in the entire process. The critical elements are that judgements to credit items are made and scoring conducted by persons who know what they are doing. These persons should be professionally trained in testing techniques or need to be trained and checked out on the Grid by someone who is professionally trained. In addition, it is important to choose informants who are sufficiently knowledgeable about the client to answer detailed questions about that person's skills.

A Grid assessment may be conducted by a combination of four primary methods. These four methods and a table illustrating their combinations follow:

Table 1

Combination of Methods
for Administering the Grid

Interview	Independent	
Interview Complete	Independent Complete	Complete
Interview Update	Independent Update	Update

Interview Method

A psychologist or other trained person interviews others who know the client well. The interviewer credits items based upon the informants' answers to questions. The informants usually read Grid items along with the interviewer. Questionable items are left blank until they can be tested. When possible, the testing takes place at the time of the interview assessment.

Independent Method

Staff persons (teachers, recreational therapists, direct-service personnel, etc.) who work with the client independently conduct their own assessment of Grid areas or items with which they are knowledgeable. These independent assessments are then sent to a psychologist or other trained person for compilation, checking, correcting, and scoring. It is important that the persons doing their own independent assessments have prior instruction in the crediting and testing of items. Also, it is important that persons conducting independent assessments refrain from guessing on questionable items. Questionable items either should be left blank for later testing or tested at the time of the independent assessment.

Complete Assessment

The assessment is conducted from the beginning starting with a blank Assessment Record. Each assessment is conducted as if it is the first Grid assessment ever conducted for the client.

Update Assessment

The Grid assessment is conducted by taking the most recent assessment for the client and updating it. Updating is accomplished by reviewing and retesting selected items and then adding or deleting items on the previous assessment. All blank items are assessed following the steps outlined in the Instructions section of this manual. Credited items are only reassessed at the upper end of each skill cluster.

The question frequently arises as to whether a client should be penalized for an item when the performance of the item is prevented by a physical handicap such as blindness, deafness, non-ambulatory condition, non-verbal condition, etc. All of these handicapping conditions reduce a person's effective adaptive behavior. Therefore, it is reasonable that a client's adaptive behavior score/rating should reflect such handicapping factors. However, should a person learn to compensate for the handicap and perform the skill in a different manner, then in many cases, crediting the item is justified. For example, if a non-verbal person learns to communicate by using formal sign language, then items involving verbal expressive communication may be credited depending upon the sophistication of the sign language and the requirements of the item. The important thing when crediting an item is that the essential intent of the item is not sacrificed.

The following Instructions summarize the steps for conducting a Grid assessment. Samples of scored Grids are included after the Instructions.

Instructions

1. Conduct Grid ratings by using one or more informants who know the person being rated well. Questionable items should be tested directly.

2. In specific skill clusters, start looking at items at about the level where you think a person is at. For example, compared to normal persons, if the person being rated seems most like a three year old, start the rating with the skills listed at the three year level of the Grid.

3. Go through all five skills listed at the level where you started, and check off each skill that a person does in the Assessment Record. Consult the Skill Cluster Descriptions for detailed descriptions of the skills being assessed. Unless stated otherwise, items credited should represent the client's common or typical performance.

4. The basal level is established by continuing to check the skills that the client has in successively lower levels until the level is reached where all five skills are checked.

5. The ceiling level is established by continuing to check the skills that the client has in successively higher levels until the level is reached where none of the five skills are checked.

6. You may wish to assume that the client possesses all the skills listed below the basal and none above the ceiling. However, there are exceptions to these assumptions; and a double basal and ceiling provides greater assurance that none of the client's skills listed in the Grid are overlooked.

7. The skills checked in the Assessment Record are then transferred to the Grid Report Form. The boxes corresponding to the checked skill items are X'd or shaded. Partial credit (half credit) may be given for items that are nearly but not quite mastered. Half credit is usually indicated by making a diagonal line in the box, with or without shading half of the box.

8. Developmental levels are computed by assigning values to each skill item. For example, all of the five skills at the 3-month level should add up to 3 months. Therefore, assign a value of 0.05 years to each item. At the 3-month and 6-month levels, the client receives credit for any blank skill items unless none of the skills have been checked at that level.

9. The values for each skill item at their respective levels are as follows:

3 months 0.05 yr.	12 months 0.1 yr.	3 years 0.2 yr.
6 months 0.05 yr.	18 months 0.1 yr.	4 years 0.2 yr.
	2 years 0.1 yr.	5 years 0.2 yr.
8 years 0.6 yr.	12 years 0.8 yr.	
	16 years 0.8 yr.	

10. The average developmental level (ADL) is computed by summing the levels of all ten skill clusters and dividing by ten. The answer is rounded off to the nearest tenth.

GRID

Lakeland Village Adaptive Behavior

REPORT FORM

AVERAGE DEVELOPMENTAL LEVEL: **2.0**

	03 MO	06 MO	12 MO	18 MO	02 YR	03 YR	04 YR	05 YR	08 YR	12 YR	16 YR	LEVEL
1. EATING	a|b|c|d|e	a|b|c|d|e	a|b|c|d|e	a|b|c|d|e		d	a|b		a|b|c|d|e	a|b|c|d|e	a|b|c|d|e	3.4 1.
2. TOILETING	a|b|c|d|e	a|b|c|d|e		e	e	b	b|c|d|e	a|b|c|d|e	a|b|c|d|e	a|b|c|d|e	a|b|c|d|e	2.8 2.
3. DRESSING	a|b|c|d|e	a|b|c|d|e	a|b|c|d|e	a|b|c|d|e		d|e	a c|d|e	a|b|c|d|e	a|b|c|d|e	a|b|c|d|e	a|b|c|d|e	2.8 3.
4. HEALTH & GROOMING	a|b|c|d|e	a|b|c|d|e		c	a|b d|e	a|b|c e	a|b|c|d|e	a|b|c|d|e	a|b|c|d|e	a|b|c|d|e	a|b|c|d|e	1.7 4.
5. COMMUNI-CATION		e	c e	a|b|c|d	a|b|c|d|e	a|b|c|d|e	a|b|c|d|e	a|b|c|d|e	a|b|c|d|e	a|b|c|d|e	a|b|c|d|e	0.85 5.
6. MOBILITY & DEXTERITY	a|b|c|d|e	a|b|c|d|e		b	b	b|c	a c	a c e	a|b|c|d|e	a|b|c|d|e	a|b|c|d|e	3.5 6.
7. VOCATION & RECREATION	a|b|c|d|e		b|c e	a|b e	a c e	a|b|c|d|e	a|b|c|d|e	a|b|c|d|e	a|b|c|d|e	a|b|c|d|e	a|b|c|d|e	0.9 7.
8. SOCIALI-ZATION	a|b|c|d|e		c|d		a c e	a|b|c|d|e	a|b|c|d|e	a|b|c|d|e	a|b|c|d|e	a|b|c|d|e	a|b|c|d|e	1.4 8.
9. ORIENTATION	a|b|c|d|e		d|a	d|e	a d|e	a|b|c|d|e	a|b|c|d|e	a|b|c|d|e	a|b|c|d|e	a|b|c|d|e	a|b|c|d|e	1.1 9.
10. SELF DIRECTION	a|b|c|d|e	a		c e	c e	a c e	a|b|c|d|e	a|b|c|d|e	a|b|c|d|e	a|b|c|d|e	a|b|c|d|e	1.7 10.

NAME: _CLIENT PROFOUNDLY RETARDED IN ADAPTIVE BEHAVIOR_   AGE: _18-11_   DATE: _____

COMMENTS: _____

GRID

LV — Lakeland Village
Adaptive Behavior

REPORT FORM

AVERAGE DEVELOPMENTAL LEVEL: **5.2**

	03 MO	06 MO	12 MO	18 MO	02 YR	03 YR	04 YR	05 YR	08 YR	12 YR	16 YR	LEVEL
1. EATING	a|b|c|d|e	a|b|c|d|e	a|b|c|d|e	a|b|c|d|e	a|b|c|d|e	a|b|c|d|e	a|b|c|d|e		b|c|d|e	a|b|c|d|e	a|b|c|d|e	5.6
2. TOILETING	a|b|c|d|e	a|b|c|d|e	a|b|c|d|e	a|b|c|d|e	a|b|c|d|e	a|b|c|d|e	a|b|c|d|e		b|d	a|b|c|d|e	a|b|c|d|e	6.8
3. DRESSING	a|b|c|d|e	a|b|c|d|e	a|b|c|d|e	a|b|c|d|e	a|b|c|d|e	a|b|c|d|e	a|b|c|d|e		c|d	a|b|c|d|e	a|b|c|d|e	6.8
4. HEALTH & GROOMING	a|b|c|d|e	a|b|c|d|e	a|b|c|d|e	a|b|c|d|e	a|b|c|d|e	a|b|c|d|e	a|b|c|d|e		a|b|c|d	a|b|c|d|e	a|b|c|d|e	5.6
5. COMMUNICATION	a|b|c|d|e	a|b|c|d|e	a|b|c|d|e	a|b|c|d|e		a	a	a|c|e	a|b|c|d|e	a|b|c|d|e	a|b|c|d|e	4.0
6. MOBILITY & DEXTERITY	a|b|c|d|e	a|b|c|d|e	a|b|c|d|e	a|b|c|d|e	a|b|c|d|e		b	b|d	c|d	a|b|c|d|e	a|b|c|d|e	6.2
7. VOCATION & RECREATION	a|b|c|d|e	a|b|c|d|e	a|b|c|d|e	a|b|c|d|e	a|b|c|d|e		c|e	b|e	a|b|c|d|e	a|b|c|d|e	a|b|c|d|e	4.2
8. SOCIALIZATION	a|b|c|d|e	a|b|c|d|e	a|b|c|d|e	a|b|c|d|e	a|b|c|d|e		a		a|b|c|d|e	a|b|c|d|e	a|b|c|d|e	4.8
9. ORIENTATION	a|b|c|d|e	a|b|c|d|e	a|b|c|d|e	a|b|c|d|e	a|b|c|d|e		e|a|b	e	a|b|c|d|e	a|b|c|d|e	a|b|c|d|e	4.2
10. SELF DIRECTION	a|b|c|d|e	a|b|c|d|e	a|b|c|d|e	a|b|c|d|e	a|b|c|d|e		e	b|c	a|b|c|d|e	a|b|c|d|e	a|b|c|d|e	4.2

NAME: CLIENT SEVERELY RETARDED IN ADAPTIVE BEHAVIOR   AGE: 13-11   DATE: _____

COMMENTS: _____

GRID

Lakeland Village Adaptive Behavior

REPORT FORM

AVERAGE DEVELOPMENTAL LEVEL: **7.4**

	03 MO	06 MO	12 MO	18 MO	02 YR	03 YR	04 YR	05 YR	08 YR	12 YR	16 YR	LEVEL
1. EATING	a|b|c|d|e	a|b|c|d|e	a|b|c|d|e	a|b|c|d|e	a|b|c|d|e	a|b|c|d|e	a|b|c|d|e		b|d	c|d|e	a|b|c|d|e	8.4
2. TOILETING	a|b|c|d|e	a|b|c|d|e	a|b|c|d|e	a|b|c|d|e	a|b|c|d|e	a|b|c|d|e	a|b|c|d|e		b	a|d	a|b|c|d|e	9.8
3. DRESSING	a|b|c|d|e	a|b|c|d|e	a|b|c|d|e	a|b|c|d|e	a|b|c|d|e	a|b|c|d|e	a|b|c|d|e	a|b|c|d|e		a|d	a|b|c|d|e	10.4
4. HEALTH & GROOMING	a|b|c|d|e	a|b|c|d|e	a|b|c|d|e	a|b|c|d|e	a|b|c|d|e	a|b|c|d|e	a|b|c|d|e		a|c|d	a|e	a|b|c|d|e	8.6
5. COMMUNI-CATION	a|b|c|d|e	a|b|c|d|e	a|b|c|d|e	a|b|c|d|e	a|b|c|d|e	a|b|c|d|e	a|b	a|b	a|b|c|d|e	a|b|c|d|e	a|b|c|d|e	4.6
6. MOBILITY & DEXTERITY	a|b|c|d|e	a|b|c|d|e	a|b|c|d|e	a|b|c|d|e	a|b|c|d|e	a|b|c|d|e	a|b	a|b|c|d|e	a|b|c|d|e	a|b|c|d|e	a|b|c|d|e	3.6
7. VOCATION & RECREATION	a|b|c|d|e	a|b|c|d|e	a|b|c|d|e	a|b|c|d|e	a|b|c|d|e	a|b|c|d|e	a|b|c|d|e		c|d	b|c|d	a|b|c|d|e	8.4
8. SOCIALI-ZATION	a|b|c|d|e	a|b|c|d|e	a|b|c|d|e	a|b|c|d|e	a|b|c|d|e	a|b|c|d|e	a|b|c|d|e	a|b|c|d|e	a|b|c|d|e	a|c|d|e	a|b|c|d|e	8.8
9. ORIENTATION	a|b|c|d|e	a|b|c|d|e	a|b|c|d|e	a|b|c|d|e	a|b|c|d|e		a	b	a|c	a|c|d|e	a|b|c|d|e	4.6
10. SELF DIRECTION	a|b|c|d|e	a|b|c|d|e	a|b|c|d|e	a|b|c|d|e	a|b|c|d|e	a|b|c|d|e	a|b|c|d|e		a|b|c|d|e	a|b|c|d|e	a|b|c|d|e	6.8

NAME: _CLIENT MODERATELY RETARDED IN ADAPTIVE BEHAVIOR_   AGE: _33-11_   DATE: _____

COMMENTS: _____

GRID
LV — Lakeland Village Adaptive Behavior
REPORT FORM

AVERAGE DEVELOPMENTAL LEVEL: **9.8**

	03 MO	06 MO	12 MO	18 MO	02 YR	03 YR	04 YR	05 YR	08 YR	12 YR	16 YR	LEVEL
1. EATING	a|b|c|d|e	a|b|c|d|e	a|b|c|d|e	a|b|c|d|e	a|b|c|d|e	a|b|c|d|e	a|b|c|d|e	a|b|c|d|e		c|d|e	a|b|c|d|e	9.6
2. TOILETING	a|b|c|d|e	a|b|c|d|e	a|b|c|d|e	a|b|c|d|e	a|b|c|d|e	a|b|c|d|e	a|b|c|d|e	a|b|c|d|e		d	a|b|c|d|e	11.2
3. DRESSING	a|b|c|d|e	a|b|c|d|e	a|b|c|d|e	a|b|c|d|e	a|b|c|d|e	a|b|c|d|e	a|b|c|d|e	a|b|c|d|e	a|b|c|d|e		b|c|d	13.6
4. HEALTH & GROOMING	a|b|c|d|e	a|b|c|d|e	a|b|c|d|e	a|b|c|d|e	a|b|c|d|e	a|b|c|d|e	a|b|c|d|e	a|b|c|d|e		a	e	a|b|c	11.2
5. COMMUNICATION	a|b|c|d|e	a|b|c|d|e	a|b|c|d|e	a|b|c|d|e	a|b|c|d|e	a|b|c|d|e	a|b|c|d|e	a|b|c|d|e	a|b|c|d|e	a|b|c|d|e	a|b|c|d|e	5.0
6. MOBILITY & DEXTERITY	a|b|c|d|e	a|b|c|d|e	a|b|c|d|e	a|b|c|d|e	a|b|c|d|e	a|b|c|d|e	a|b|c|d|e	a|b|c|d|e		d|e	b|c|d|e	11.2
7. VOCATION & RECREATION	a|b|c|d|e	a|b|c|d|e	a|b|c|d|e	a|b|c|d|e	a|b|c|d|e	a|b|c|d|e	a|b|c|d|e		c|e	c|d|e	a|b|c|d|e	8.4
8. SOCIALIZATION	a|b|c|d|e	a|b|c|d|e	a|b|c|d|e	a|b|c|d|e	a|b|c|d|e	a|b|c|d|e	a|b|c|d|e		a|c|d	e	d|e	10.8
9. ORIENTATION	a|b|c|d|e	a|b|c|d|e	a|b|c|d|e	a|b|c|d|e	a|b|c|d|e	a|b|c|d|e	a|b|c|d|e	a|b|c|d|e	a|c|d	a|b|c|d|e	a|b|c|d|e	7.0
10. SELF DIRECTION	a|b|c|d|e	a|b|c|d|e	a|b|c|d|e	a|b|c|d|e	a|b|c|d|e	a|b|c|d|e	a|b|c|d|e	a|b|c|d|e	a	a|c|d	a|b|c|d|e	9.6

NAME: _CLIENT MILDLY RETARDED IN ADAPTIVE BEHAVIOR_ AGE: _38-11_ DATE: _____

COMMENTS: _____

LV GRID

Lakeland Village Adaptive Behavior

REPORT FORM

AVERAGE DEVELOPMENTAL LEVEL: **14.2**

	03 MO	06 MO	12 MO	18 MO	02 YR	03 YR	04 YR	05 YR.	08 YR.	12 YR.	16 YR.	LEVEL
1. EATING	a|b|c|d|e	a|b|c|d|e	a|b|c|d|e	a|b|c|d|e	a|b|c|d|e	a|b|c|d|e	a|b|c|d|e	a|b|c|d|e	a|b|c|d|e		b|c|d	13.6
2. TOILETING	a|b|c|d|e	a|b|c|d|e	a|b|c|d|e	a|b|c|d|e	a|b|c|d|e	a|b|c|d|e	a|b|c|d|e	a|b|c|d|e	a|b|c|d|e		b|d|e	13.6
3. DRESSING	a|b|c|d|e	a|b|c|d|e	a|b|c|d|e	a|b|c|d|e	a|b|c|d|e	a|b|c|d|e	a|b|c|d|e	a|b|c|d|e	a|b|c|d|e		d	15.2
4. HEALTH & GROOMING	a|b|c|d|e	a|b|c|d|e	a|b|c|d|e	a|b|c|d|e	a|b|c|d|e	a|b|c|d|e	a|b|c|d|e	a|b|c|d|e	a|b|c|d|e		a|b|c|e	12.8
5. COMMUNICATION	a|b|c|d|e	a|b|c|d|e	a|b|c|d|e	a|b|c|d|e	a|b|c|d|e	a|b|c|d|e	a|b|c|d|e	a|b|c|d|e	a|b|c|d|e		b|c|d|e	12.8
6. MOBILITY & DEXTERITY	a|b|c|d|e	a|b|c|d|e	a|b|c|d|e	a|b|c|d|e	a|b|c|d|e	a|b|c|d|e	a|b|c|d|e	a|b|c|d|e	a|b|c|d|e		a|d|e	13.6
7. VOCATION & RECREATION	a|b|c|d|e	a|b|c|d|e	a|b|c|d|e	a|b|c|d|e	a|b|c|d|e	a|b|c|d|e	a|b|c|d|e	a|b|c|d|e	a|b|c|d|e		e	15.2
8. SOCIALIZATION	a|b|c|d|e	a|b|c|d|e	a|b|c|d|e	a|b|c|d|e	a|b|c|d|e	a|b|c|d|e	a|b|c|d|e	a|b|c|d|e	a|b|c|d|e		a|b	14.4
9. ORIENTATION	a|b|c|d|e	a|b|c|d|e	a|b|c|d|e	a|b|c|d|e	a|b|c|d|e	a|b|c|d|e	a|b|c|d|e	a|b|c|d|e	a|b|c|d|e		b|d	14.4
10. SELF DIRECTION	a|b|c|d|e	a|b|c|d|e	a|b|c|d|e	a|b|c|d|e	a|b|c|d|e	a|b|c|d|e	a|b|c|d|e	a|b|c|d|e	a|b|c|d|e	a|b|c|d|e		16.0

NAME: CLIENT NOT RETARDED IN ADAPTIVE BEHAVIOR   AGE: 51-11   DATE: _____

COMMENTS: _____

LAKELAND VILLAGE

ADAPTIVE BEHAVIOR GRID
(1984 Revision)

ASSESSMENT RECORD

NAME _____ SEX _____

RESIDENCE/ADDRESS _____

| _____ | _____ | _____ | ASSESSMENT DATE | ___ | ___ | ___ |
| (MA/IQ) | (MI CLASS) | (DATE) | | (yr) | (mo) | (day) |

| _____ | _____ | _____ | BIRTHDATE | ___ | ___ | ___ |
| (ADL) | (AB CLASS) | (DATE) | | (yr) | (mo) | (day) |

RECORDER _____

INFORMANT (S) _____ AGE _____

PHYSICAL/SENSORY HANDICAPS _____

INSTRUCTIONS FOR ADMINISTRATION AND SCORING

1. Conduct Grid ratings by using one or more informants who know the person being rated well. Questionable items should be tested directly.

2. In specific skill clusters, start looking at items at about the level where you think a person is at. For example, compared to normal persons, if the person being rated seems most like a three year old, start the rating with the skills listed at the three year level of the Grid.

3. Go through all five skills listed at the level where you started, and check off each skill that a person does in the Assessment Record. Consult the Skill Cluster Descriptions for detailed descriptions of the skills being assessed. Unless stated otherwise, items credited should represent the client's common or typical performance.

4. The basal level is established by continuing to check the skills that the client has in successively lower levels until the level is reached where all of the five skills are checked.

5. The ceiling level is established by continuing to check the skills that the client has in successively higher levels until the level is reached where none of the five skills are checked.

6. You may wish to assume that the client possesses all the skills listed below, the basal and none above the ceiling. However, there are exceptions to these assumptions; and a double basal and ceiling provides greater assurance that none of the client's skills listed in the Grid are overlooked.

7. The skills checked in the Assessment Record are then transferred to the Grid Report Form. The boxes corresponding to the checked skill items are X'd or shaded. Partial credit (half credit) may be given for items that are nearly but not quite mastered. Half credit is usually indicated by making a diagonal line in the box, with or without shading half of the box.

8. Developmental levels are computed by assigning values to each skill item. For example, all of the five skills at the 3-month level should add up to 3 months. therefore, assign a value of 0.05 years to each item. At the 3-month and 6-month levels, the client receives credit for any blank skill items unless none of the skills have been checked at that level.

9. The values for each skill item at their respective levels are as follows:

3 months 0.05 yr.	12 months 0.1 yr.	3 years 0.2 yr.	8 years 0.6 yr.	12 years 0.8 yr.
6 months 0.05 yr.	18 months 0.1 yr.	4 years 0.2 yr.		16 years 0.8 yr.
	2 years 0.1 yr.	5 years 0.2 yr.		

10. The average developmental level (ADL) is computed by summing the levels of all ten skill clusters and dividing by ten. The answer is rounded off to the nearest tenth.

Eating   # Toileting

Eating	Age	(✓)	Toileting	(✓)
A. Opens mouth when lips are touched by spoon B. Swallows food placed on back of tongue C. Opens mouth when lips are touched by cup D. Sucks liquid from bottle E. Sips from cup held by another	03 Mo. (.05)	A ☐ B ☐ C ☐ D ☐ E ☐	A. Sits on toilet with considerable support B. Shows pattern for bowel movements C. Eliminates occasionally if placed on toilet (BM)	A ☐ B ☐ C ☐ D ☐ E ☐
A. Reaches forward for spoon with head B. Sucks food from spoon held by another C. Holds spoon in palmar grasp D. Lifts cup by handle E. Drinks from cup held by another	06 Mo. (.05)	A ☐ B ☐ C ☐ D ☐ E ☐	A. Sits on toilet with little support B. Remains dry for one hour C. Eliminates at end of dry period if toileted.	A ☐ B ☐ C ☐ D ☐ E ☐
A. Opens mouth when spoon is presented B. Chews some food before swallowing C. Feeds self with fingers D. Places spoon in bowl in imitation E. Holds cup in two hands and drinks with some spilling	12 Mo. (.10)	A ☐ B ☐ C ☐ D ☐ E ☐	A. Sits on toilet when left alone B. Wakes up dry from sleep C. Urinates after awakening D. Eliminates if toileted at customary time (BM) E. Shows signs of discomfort when wet or soiled	A ☐ B ☐ C ☐ D ☐ E ☐
A. Pushes spoon into food with partial physical assistance B. Holds spoon horizontally as raised to mouth C. Tilts spoon up, removes food with upper lip D. Removes from mouth objects too big to swallow E. Holds cup in two hands and drinks with little spilling	18 Mo. (.10)	A ☐ B ☐ C ☐ D ☐ E ☐	A. Stays dry most of day when toileted B. Reports accidents by word, sound, etc. C. Goes into bathroom when directed D. Requests toilet by word or gesture E. Responds to question as to need for toilet	A ☐ B ☐ C ☐ D ☐ E ☐
A. Fills spoon and raises without using free hand B. Wipes face with napkin (not effective) C. Unwraps packaged food D. Rejects inedible substances E. Sets down glass with one hand or uses straw	02 Yr. (.10)	A ☐ B ☐ C ☐ D ☐ E ☐	A. Verbalizes or gestures toilet need B. Places self on toilet when directed C. Indicates when finished on toilet D. Takes off wet pants E. Pushes down own pants when toileted	A ☐ B ☐ C ☐ D ☐ E ☐
A. Spears food with fork, carries food to mouth B. Carries spoon, without turning it, to mouth C. Eats meal without using fingers D. Gets drink without assistance E. Holds cup by handle or pauses between sips	03 Yr. (.20)	A ☐ B ☐ C ☐ D ☐ E ☐	A. Places self on toilet alone B. Wipes self when told C. Flushes toilet alone D. Remains dry at night when routinely awakened E. Manages own clothing in toileting situation with help	A ☐ B ☐ C ☐ D ☐ E ☐
A. Cuts food with fork B. Uses spoon and fork properly C. Tests food temperature and blows to cool D. Serves self "easy" foods with little spilling E. Gets snack without assistance	04 Yr. (.20)	A ☐ B ☐ C ☐ D ☐ E ☐	A. Uses toilet on own initiative B. Wipes self with reminders C. Remains dry at night D. Washes hands after toileting when verbally prompted E. Manages own clothing in toileting situation without help	A ☐ B ☐ C ☐ D ☐ E ☐
A. Cuts soft food with knife B. Spreads butter with knife C. Serves self "hard" foods with little spilling D. Obtains ingredients and prepares sandwich E. Displays manners when directed	05 Yr. (.20)	A ☐ B ☐ C ☐ D ☐ E ☐	A. Handles toileting in strange setting with aid B. Wipes self adequately C. Flushes toilet on own initiative D. Washes hands after toileting E. Adjusts clothing before leaving lavatory	A ☐ B ☐ C ☐ D ☐ E ☐
A. Cuts meat with knife and fork B. Uses can opener C. Chooses reasonable amounts of food D. Prepares food (soup) following routine E. Displays manners when prompted	08 Yr. (.60)	A ☐ B ☐ C ☐ D ☐ E ☐	A. Uses toilet before going out B. Distinguishes sex identification signs C. Closes door while using toilet D. Uses toilet seat protector when reminded E. Uses soap and towel dispensers	A ☐ B ☐ C ☐ D ☐ E ☐
A. Tests and seasons food to taste B. Displays manners with few reminders C. Makes balanced meal using pictures of food D. Prepares food following recipes E. Considers cost when ordering from menu	12 Yr. (.80)	A ☐ B ☐ C ☐ D ☐ E ☐	A. Locates restroom in unfamiliar places B. Uses locks and latches to insure privacy C. Cleans up after self before leaving bathroom in home D. Uses bathroom correctly when visiting E. Uses toilet seat protector independently	A ☐ B ☐ C ☐ D ☐ E ☐
A. Knows how to prevent and detect food spoilage B. Plans, buys, fixes, and serves adequate meal C. Knows simple nutrition facts D. Plans complete and adequate three-day menu E. Considers cost, orders, and pays for meal out	16 Yr. (.80)	A ☐ B ☐ C ☐ D ☐ E ☐	A. Explains the importance of regularity B. Understands common treatments of irregularity C. Describes symptoms of serious elimination problems D. Explains unusual toileting circumstances E. Demonstrates methods for correcting malfunctioning toilet	A ☐ B ☐ C ☐ D ☐ E ☐

DEVELOPMENTAL LEVEL _____   DEVELOPMENTAL LEVEL _____

19

Dressing | Health and Grooming

03 Mo. (.05)

Dressing (✔)
- A Manipulates bedcover with hands
- B Manipulates own clothing with hands
- C Anticipates dressing and undressing
- D
- E

Health and Grooming (✔)
- A Lies in shallow bath, partly supports head
- B Sits in bath when supported
- C Cooperates while in bath
- D Closes eyes when face is washed
- E Grasps washcloth placed in hand

06 Mo. (.05)

Dressing
- A Removes foot coverings
- B Manipulates discrete parts of clothing
- C Cooperates actively when dressed and undressed
- D
- E

Health and Grooming
- A Sits in bath with little support
- B Closes eyes when approached by washcloth
- C Grasps washcloth within reach
- D Lies in shallow bath, completely supports head
- E

12 Mo. (.10)

Dressing
- A Removes socks or untied shoes.
- B Pulls off pants
- C Directs arm into armhole
- D Extends leg to have pants put on
- E Imitates putting on hat

Health and Grooming
- A Places hands in water when assisted
- B Touches face with washcloth when assisted
- C Puts soap on soapdish when assisted
- D Touches head with comb when assisted
- E Puts toothbrush in mouth when assisted

18 Mo. (.10)

Dressing
- A Directs toe into shoe
- B Removes unbuttoned jacket or shirt
- C Takes off mittens or gloves
- D Directs leg into pant leg
- E Unzips easy zipper

Health and Grooming
- A Makes handwashing motion when requested
- B Wipes face with washcloth when requested
- C Blows nose when hanky is held to it
- D Picks up comb and "combs" hair upon request
- E Applies soap to hands

02 Yr. (.10)

Dressing
- A Removes untied shoes when verbally prompted
- B Pushes down pants when verbally prompted
- C Pulls up pants once started
- D Attempts to put on pants without help
- E Finds armholes and thrusts arms into them

Health and Grooming
- A Tries to wash hands with soap and water
- B Tries to dry hands
- C Comes when called for health and grooming activities
- D Applies soap to body parts
- E Puts toothbrush in mouth and "brushes"

03 Yr. (.20)

Dressing
- A Tries to put on shoes and socks
- B Undresses with help on fasteners only
- C Dresses self in wardrobe already laid out
- D Fetches clothing article from storage
- E Unbuttons front buttons

Health and Grooming
- A Indicates when sick or injured
- B Dries own hand effectively
- C Blows and wipes nose when reminded
- D Avoids hazards or dangers
- E Puts toothpaste on toothbrush

04 Yr. (.20)

Dressing
- A Puts on socks with heels down
- B Distinguishes front from back of garments
- C Dresses self with little assistance
- D Laces shoes
- E Buttons front buttons

Health and Grooming
- A Washes hands effectively
- B Dries most of self
- C Washes self effectively
- D Avoids eating food dropped on floor
- E Brushes teeth with directions

05 Yr. (.20)

Dressing
- A Puts shoes on correct feet
- B Turns slipcover garment right-side-out
- C Places clothes in appropriate drawers
- D Unties loose knots
- E Buckles and unbuckles belts, shoes or galoshes

Health and Grooming
- A Localizes site of discomfort
- B Bathes self when supervised
- C Keeps nose clean
- D Combs hair so it falls in one direction
- E Adjusts water temperature

08 Yr. (.60)

Dressing
- A Changes clothes as required by routine
- B Helps select new clothes
- C Selects clothing suitable to weather
- D Keeps shoelaces tied without reminder
- E Zips jacket zippers without help

Health and Grooming
- A Treats minor illness or injury
- B Performs complete bathing sequence
- C Cuts own fingernails
- D Shampoos and combs hair adequately
- E Brushes own teeth

12 Yr. (.80)

Dressing
- A Shines shoes or washes socks
- B Picks new clothes with advice
- C Selects garments appropriate to occasion
- D Tries on clothes before buying
- E Hangs clothes up on hangers

Health and Grooming
- A Takes own medication for short intervals
- B Recognizes symptoms of illness
- C Maintains body cleanliness
- D Maintains satisfactory dental hygiene
- E Answers simple questions about reproduction

16 Yr. (.80)

Dressing
- A Washes, dries, and irons clothing
- B Budgets for and buys wardrobe
- C Prepares list of needed clothing
- D Performs simple mending
- E Maintains orderly clothing area

Health and Grooming
- A Takes responsibiltiy for own medications
- B Arranges and reports for medical appointments
- C Answers basic questions about first aid
- D Maintains acceptable appearance
- E Answers questions about VD and pregnancy prevention

DEVELOPMENTAL LEVEL _____   DEVELOPMENTAL LEVEL _____

	Communicating				Mobility and Dexterity	

Communicating   ## Mobility and Dexterity

		(✓)			
Attends to environmental sounds	A	**03 Mo.**	Follows object or sound	A	
Attends to environmental sights	B		Reaches for dangling object	B	
Vocalizes two different sounds	C		Holds object placed in hand	C	
Communicates basic needs	D	**(.05)**	Supports upper body with arms	D	
Vocalizes when talked to	E		Holds head steady	E	
Makes noise with objects	A	**06 Mo.**	Stands with support	A	
Turns head toward sound	B		Handles objects	B	
Vocalizes several different sounds	C		Moves backward or forward on abdomen	C	
Communicates wants	D	**(.05)**	Rolls from back to stomach	D	
Repeats own sound when sound is imitated	E		Sits with little support	E	
Identifies one common object	A	**12 Mo.**	Stands alone without assistance	A	
Attends when directed	B		Transfers small objects using pincer grasp	B	
Says two words	C		Performs fine motor tasks of 12-month level complexity	C	
Indicates wants	D	**(.10)**	Stands or sits independently	D	
Imitates words or gestures	E		Ambulates by walking or creeping	E	
Points to pictures of objects	A	**18 Mo.**	Runs poorly or walks well	A	
Uses gestures to help reinforce language	B		Propels ball in forward direction	B	
Says ten words	C		Performs fine motor tasks of 18-month level complexity	C	
Uses words for wants	D	**(.10)**	Seats self on chair	D	
Responds to simple directions	E		Walks up stairs assisted	E	
Scores at 2-year level on picture vocabulary test	A	**02 Yr.**	Runs or jumps without falling	A	
Listens to stories	B		Balances on board or when crouching	B	
Names familiar things	C		Performs fine motor tasks of 2-year level complexity	C	
Says two-word sentences	D	**(.10)**	Opens door	D	
Uses pronouns	E		Walks up stairs unaided or down stairs aided	E	
Scores at 3-year level on picture vocabulary test	A	**03 Yr.**	Stands or hops on one foot	A	
Answers simple questions	B		Rides a pedal toy	B	
Gives simple account of experience	C		Performs fine motor tasks of 3-year level complexity	C	
Recites part of song or rhyme	D	**(.20)**	Throws object with some accuracy	D	
Performs academic skills at nursery school level	E		Alternates feet going up stairs	E	
Scores at 4-year level on picture vocabulary test	A	**04 Yr.**	Gallops or performs standing or running jump	A	
Tells use of common objects	B		Walks a line without stepping off	B	
Says five-word long sentences	C		Performs fine motor tasks of 4-year level complexiy	C	
Repeats nine-word long sentences	D	**(.20)**	Carries cup of water or catches ball	D	
Performs academic skills at the pre-kindergarten level	E		Alternates feet going down stairs	E	
Scores at 5-year level on picture vocabulary test	A	**05 Yr.**	Skips correctly or hops on one foot	A	
Asks questions to seek information	B		Walks on board	B	
Gives detailed account of experience	C		Performs fine motor tasks of 5-year level complexity	C	
Defines simple words	D	**(.20)**	Balances on toes or one foot	D	
Performs academic skills at the kindergarten level	E		Runs 35 yards or kicks ball through air	E	
Scores at 8-year level on picture vocabulary test	A	**08 Yr.**	Hits ball with bat, racquet, or paddle	A	
States how objects are alike and not alike	B		Balances on bicycle or skates	B	
Reads and uses simple instructions	C		Writes or prints legible words and sentences	C	
Uses telephone routinely	D	**(.60)**	Demonstrates the crawl swimming stroke	D	
Performs academic skills at 3rd grade level	E		Bounces and catches ball with one hand	E	
Reads for information and enjoyment	A	**12 Yr.**	Plays musical instrument	A	
Writes short, meaningful letters	B		Throws softball	B	
Describes a story in length with detail	C		Pulls up or hangs on a bar	C	
Finds alphabetically indexed information	D	**(.80)**	Performs standing broad jump	D	
Performs academic skills at the 7th grade level	E		Performs 50-yard dash	E	
Discusses abstract and philosophical ideas	A	**16 Yr.**	Participates in competitive sport	A	
Writes business letters	B		Ties several different knots	B	
Reads and uses complex instructions	C		Operates device requiring complex skills	C	
Delivers formal speech	D	**(.80)**	Dances with another person	D	
Performs academic skills at the 10th grade level	E		Qualifies for driving automobile	E	

DEVELOPMENTAL LEVEL _____   DEVELOPMENTAL LEVEL _____

Vocation and Recreation

	(✓)
Inspects surroundings within room	A ☐
Shows interest in dangling object	B ☐
Anticipates return of toy	C ☐
Engages in non-directed physical activities	D ☐
Plays with fingers	E ☐
Inspects and manipulates	A ☐
Reaches promptly for seen objects	B ☐
Entertains self unattended for 15 minutes	C ☐
Engages in gross motor exercises	D ☐
Engages in play with toys	E ☐
Watches scenery on excursions	A ☐
Imitates simple demonstrations	B ☐
Plays unattended for 30 minutes with toys	C ☐
Plays unattended for 30 mins. in gross motor exercises	D ☐
Plays with several small objects at one time	E ☐
Points to objects of interest	A ☐
Imitates domestic tasks	B ☐
Plays alone for up to 60 minutes	C ☐
Performs simple tasks in home	D ☐
Manipulates objects in intended manner	E ☐
Performs simple tasks in home	A ☐
Imitates adult tasks with toys	B ☐
Operates action toys	C ☐
Engages in gross motor play	D ☐
Engages in sedentary play	E ☐
Helps in home	A ☐
Engages in pretend play	B ☐
Engages in creative play	C ☐
Uses gross motor equipment	D ☐
Engages in sedentary activities	E ☐
Runs short errands	A ☐
Engages in dramatic play	B ☐
Plays alone for two hours	C ☐
Uses gross motor equipment	D ☐
Engages in sedentary manual tasks	E ☐
Helps about the home	A ☐
Carries out preplanned projects	B ☐
Completes activity	C ☐
Engages in gross motor activities	D ☐
Performs fine motor tasks	E ☐
Performs useful chores	A ☐
Uses simple tools	B ☐
Reads simple material for recreation	C ☐
Engages in variety of play activities	D ☐
Assembles toys	E ☐
Performs responsible tasks for pay	A ☐
Budgets allowance or earnings	B ☐
Plans and carries out project	C ☐
Performs activities requiring complex skills	D ☐
Performs simple creative work	E ☐
Performs responsible employment	A ☐
Understands essential economics	B ☐
Displays appropriate job-readiness skills	C ☐
Describes variety of jobs and requirements	D ☐
Builds or repairs with adult skill	E ☐

DEVELOPMENTAL LEVEL _____

Socialization

	(✓)
03 Mo. Indicates need for attention	A ☐
Makes eye contact	B ☐
Watches people	C ☐
(.05) Smiles responsively	D ☐
Listens to voices	E ☐
06 Mo. Indicates desire for companionship	A ☐
Responds positively to familiar persons	B ☐
Participates in social play	C ☐
(.05) Smiles in response to smile	D ☐
Distinguishes adults from children	E ☐
12 Mo. Indicates desire for companionship	A ☐
Shows affection when cued	B ☐
Participates in social games	C ☐
(.10) Participates in give-and-take play routines	D ☐
Enjoys social walks	E ☐
18 Mo. Engages in supervised parallel play	A ☐
Seeks another for specific purpose	B ☐
Participates in group activity	C ☐
(.10) Helps family member when directed	D ☐
Pretends social behavior with toys when cued	E ☐
02 Yr. Plays in parallel for 20 minutes	A ☐
Expresses affection without cues	B ☐
Initiates greetings and farewells	C ☐
(.10) Helps family members when directed	D ☐
Pretends social play with toys spontaneously	E ☐
03 Yr. Plays with peer unsupervised for 30 minutes	A ☐
Waits turn in activities	B ☐
Initiates conversations	C ☐
(.20) Entertains less capable person	D ☐
Participates in supervised group activity	E ☐
04 Yr. Plays with peer for two hours	A ☐
Shares posessions	B ☐
Converses socially during activities	C ☐
(.20) Participates in show-and-tell activities	D ☐
Plays in loosely structured group game	E ☐
05 Yr. Follows rules in supervised group games	A ☐
Prarticipates in group project	B ☐
Practices social conventions with prompting	C ☐
(.20) Helps care for less capable person	D ☐
Sings in group	E ☐
08 Yr. Participates in unsupervised group games	A ☐
Follows rules in group table games	B ☐
Practices social conventions without prompting	C ☐
(.60) Teaches less capable individual	D ☐
Dramatizes social situations	E ☐
12 Yr. Participates as a team member	A ☐
Participates in organized group acitvity	B ☐
Contributes to group discussion	C ☐
(.80) Undertakes responsible child watching tasks	D ☐
Describes the qualitites desired in a friend	E ☐
16 Yr. Plans, organizes, and executes group activities	A ☐
Participates in special interest group	B ☐
Demonstrates social courtesies without prompting	C ☐
(.80) Demonstrates acceptable dating behavior	D ☐
Reacts to novel social setting appropriately	E ☐

DEVELOPMENTAL LEVEL _____

Orientation

Skill		(✓)
Investigates self or objects	A	☐
Anticipates routine happenings	B	☐
Follows vanishing object with head	C	☐
Discriminates novel from routine experiences	D	☐
Searches with eyes for sound	E	☐
Responds positively to own mirror image	A	☐
Anticipates routine happenings	B	☐
Searches for vanishing object	C	☐
Discriminates unfamiliar person	D	☐
Explores objects	E	☐
Knows own name	A	☐
Differentiates between objects	B	☐
Retrieves hidden object	C	☐
Plays orientation games	D	☐
Differentiates between familiar persons	E	☐
Points to named body parts	A	☐
Associates future events with routines	B	☐
Shows where familiar things are kept	C	☐
Follows two of four orientation directions	D	☐
Says or gestures goodbye	E	☐
Refers to self and family by name	A	☐
Knows words denoting the future	B	☐
Identifies possessions of family members	C	☐
Follows four of four orientation directions	D	☐
Knows words denoting the present	E	☐
Gives first and last name, and sex	A	☐
Matches objects by shape or color	B	☐
Compares size of objects	C	☐
Follows directions containing prepositions	D	☐
Answers simple orientation questions	E	☐
Names several colors	A	☐
Knows when events take place	B	☐
Compares objects by weight and texture	C	☐
Performs commissions containing prepositions	D	☐
Knows living location	E	☐
Draws picture of person	A	☐
Gives opposites	B	☐
Distinguishes own right from left hand	C	☐
Knows how to get to familiar locations	D	☐
Knows age and days of the week	E	☐
Compares self to others	A	☐
Knows personal time schedule	B	☐
Understands basic conservation concepts	C	☐
Locates landmarks on a simplified map	D	☐
Knows time, months, year and season	E	☐
Knows own assets and shortcomings	A	☐
Draws a floor plan of own home	B	☐
Names extended family	C	☐
Locates state, town, and home on map	D	☐
Defines abstract orientation concepts	E	☐
Knows own potential	A	☐
Outlines plan for the future	B	☐
Estimates distance, heights, etc.	C	☐
Locates address	D	☐
Plans a trip	E	☐

DEVELOPMENTAL LEVEL _____

Self Direction

Age	Skill		(✓)
03 Mo. (.05)	Stops activity to listen to a sound	A	☐
	Quiets with change of scene	B	☐
	Repeats behavior which produces a change	C	☐
	Blinks at object near eyes	D	☐
	Quiets when attended	E	☐
06 Mo. (.05)	Removes tissue placed on face	A	☐
	Stops fussing when distracted with toy or music	B	☐
	Repeats behavior which is imitated	C	☐
	Attends to subtle stimuli	D	☐
	Inhibits behavior briefly after being stopped	E	☐
12 Mo. (.10)	Responds to social reward	A	☐
	Inhibits briefly when told no	B	☐
	Performs new movements after being assisted	C	☐
	Attends to novel stimulus	D	☐
	Cooperates with simple requests	E	☐
18 Mo. (.10)	Changes activities cooperatively if prompted	A	☐
	Stops or delays activity when given special cues	B	☐
	Imitates newly observed actions	C	☐
	Establishes eye contact when called	D	☐
	Demonstrates beginning awareness of hazards	E	☐
02 Yr. (.10)	Goes about area briefly unattended	A	☐
	Responds to a variety of inhibitory cues	B	☐
	Imitates peer behavior when cued	C	☐
	Demonstrates preference for specific items	D	☐
	Shares toy when told	E	☐
03 Yr. (.20)	Works for praise	A	☐
	Tolerates delays with promise of later	B	☐
	Performs non-preferred tasks given a reason	C	☐
	Relaxes for 10 minutes during story or music	D	☐
	Improves own behavior after group removal	E	☐
04 Yr. (.20)	Follows rules regarding boundaries	A	☐
	Works for extension of privileges	B	☐
	Improves behavior as a result of redirection	C	☐
	Demonstrates knowledge of unpleasant consequences	D	☐
	Asks permission for privileges	E	☐
05 Yr. (.20)	Changes activity with advanced warning	A	☐
	Follows kindergarten rules	B	☐
	Communicates that lying and theft are wrong	C	☐
	Hastens when told to hurry	D	☐
	Indicates own ability with some accuracy	E	☐
08 Yr. (.60)	Demonstrates ability to empathize	A	☐
	Modifies own behavior following deprivation	B	☐
	Lists rules in home, school, or community	C	☐
	Improves behavior while on token system	D	☐
	Corrects actions after viewing mistakes of others	E	☐
12 Yr. (.80)	Describes effects of stress on own behavior	A	☐
	Controls own emotional behavior	B	☐
	Describes various ethical standards	C	☐
	Weighs the pros and cons of decisions	D	☐
	Persuades others without using force	E	☐
16 Yr. (.80)	Describes forces which control own behavior	A	☐
	Describes effective self-improvement system	B	☐
	Analyzes controversial moral issues	C	☐
	Analyzes effects of action on self and others	D	☐
	Describes legal consequences of various acts	E	☐

DEVELOPMENTAL LEVEL _____

SKILL CLUSTER PROFILE

16.0
15.0
14.0
13.0
12.0
11.0
10.0
9.0
8.0
7.0
6.0
5.0
4.0
3.0
2.0
1.0

EAT TOI DRE H&G COM M&D V&R SOC ORI S-D

GRID

LV Lakeland Village Adaptive Behavior

REPORT FORM

AVERAGE DEVELOPMENTAL LEVEL [ ]

	03 MO	06 MO	12 MO	18 MO	02 YR	03 YR	04 YR	05 YR	08 YR	12 YR	16 YR	LEVEL
1. EATING	a b c d e	a b c d e	a b c d e	a b c d e	a b c d e	a b c d e	a b c d e	a b c d e	a b c d e	a b c d e	a b c d e	1.
2. TOILETING	a b c d e	a b c d e	a b c d e	a b c d e	a b c d e	a b c d e	a b c d e	a b c d e	a b c d e	a b c d e	a b c d e	2.
3. DRESSING	a b c d e	a b c d e	a b c d e	a b c d e	a b c d e	a b c d e	a b c d e	a b c d e	a b c d e	a b c d e	a b c d e	3.
4. HEALTH & GROOMING	a b c d e	a b c d e	a b c d e	a b c d e	a b c d e	a b c d e	a b c d e	a b c d e	a b c d e	a b c d e	a b c d e	4.
5. COMMUNI-CATION	a b c d e	a b c d e	a b c d e	a b c d e	a b c d e	a b c d e	a b c d e	a b c d e	a b c d e	a b c d e	a b c d e	5.
6. MOBILITY & DEXTERITY	a b c d e	a b c d e	a b c d e	a b c d e	a b c d e	a b c d e	a b c d e	a b c d e	a b c d e	a b c d e	a b c d e	6.
7. VOCATION & RECREATION	a b c d e	a b c d e	a b c d e	a b c d e	a b c d e	a b c d e	a b c d e	a b c d e	a b c d e	a b c d e	a b c d e	7.
8. SOCIALI-ZATION	a b c d e	a b c d e	a b c d e	a b c d e	a b c d e	a b c d e	a b c d e	a b c d e	a b c d e	a b c d e	a b c d e	8.
9. ORIENTATION	a b c d e	a b c d e	a b c d e	a b c d e	a b c d e	a b c d e	a b c d e	a b c d e	a b c d e	a b c d e	a b c d e	9.
10. SELF DIRECTION	a b c d e	a b c d e	a b c d e	a b c d e	a b c d e	a b c d e	a b c d e	a b c d e	a b c d e	a b c d e	a b c d e	10.

NAME: _____ AGE: _____ DATE: _____

COMMENTS: _____

EATING

03 MONTHS

EAT 03M A **Opens mouth when lips are touched by spoon**
Credit is given if the client opens mouth to accept an item of food when the spoon or food touches lips. Finger-held foods may be presented by hand.

EAT 03M B **Swallows food placed on back of tongue**
Credit is given if the client swallows small portions of food that have been pureed or have the consistency of pureed food.

EAT 03M C **Opens mouth when lips are touched by cup**
Credit is given if the client opens mouth when lips are touched by any drinking vessel including glass, cup or bottle.

EAT 03M D **Sucks liquid from bottle**
Credit is given if the client sucks liquid from a bottle with a nipple. This item should always be·credited if the client drinks liquids from a container other than a bottle.

EAT 03M E **Sips from cup held by another**
Credit is given if the client is able to swallow some liquid which is presented by cup or glass, even though spilling may be considerable.

06 MONTHS

EAT 06M A **Reaches forward for spoon with head**
Credit is given if the client moves head in direction of food item presented on spoon or with hand.

EAT 06M B **Sucks food from spoon held by another**
Credit is given if the client actively tries to remove food from a spoon which is presented and touched to lips.

EAT 06M C **Holds spoon in palmar grasp**
Credit is given if the client picks up and holds a spoon after attention is directed to the spoon. Interest in the spoon may be accomplished by tapping on plate or rattling in cup or bowl.

EAT 06M D Lifts cup by handle
Credit is given if the client manipulates a cup set within easy reach and in so doing, picks up the cup by its handle. The cup need not be picked up in an upright position.

EAT 06M E Drinks from cup held by another
Credit is given if the client drinks from a vessel held to lips without appreciable spilling.

12 MONTHS

EAT 12M A Opens mouth when spoon is presented
Credit is given if the client opens mouth at the sight of an approaching spoon laden with food.

EAT 12M B Chews some of food before swallowing
Credit is given if the client makes some chewing motions before swallowing food.

EAT 12M C Feeds self with fingers
Credit is given if the client picks up and eats food such as crackers and portions of bread without assistance.

EAT 12M D Places spoon in bowl in imitation
Credit is given if the client picks up and places a spoon in an eating container after being told to do so and given a demonstration.

EAT 12M E Holds cup in two hands and drinks with some spilling
Credit is given if the client picks up and holds a cup or glass in one or two hands and drinks unassisted. Some spilling may occur, but at least half of the container's contents should be successfully consumed.

18 MONTHS

EAT 18M A Pushes spoon into food with partial physical assistance
Credit is given if the client picks up and pushes spoon into the food, correct side up, when verbally directed and given a small amount of physical guidance.

EAT 18M B Holds spoon horizontally as raised to mouth
Credit is given if the client gets the spoon from the food to mouth without appreciably turning the spoon and by raising elbow rather than moving head down to the spoon. Verbal and gestural assistance is per-

mitted, but physical assistance should not be
necessary.

EAT 18M C **Tilts spoon up, removes food with upper lip**
Credit is given if the client, holding the spoon alone,
removes food from spoon with upper lip by tilting
handle upward and removing from mouth. Considerable spilling is allowable at this level, but at least
half of the food should end up in mouth without being
spilled. Physical assistance should not be necessary
once the spoon has reached the mouth.

EAT 18M D **Removes from mouth objects too big to swallow**
Credit is given if client removes from mouth, hard objects or food items too large to chew or swallow.
Removal should occur either spontaneously or after
gestural or verbal prompting. Parents typically elicit
this behavior by holding a hand out and requesting
that the child spit out or give them the item.

EAT 18M E **Holds cup in two hands and drinks with little spilling**
Credit is given if the client picks up and holds a cup
or glass with one or both hands and drinks
unassisted with little spilling. At least 80% of the contents should be successfully consumed.

02 YEARS

EAT 02Y A **Fills spoon and raises without using free hand**
Credit is given if the client pushes point of spoon into
food and raises spoon from food without using free
hand to push food onto spoon. The entire sequence
should be performed without physical assistance. At
least half of the food should end up in mouth without
being spilled.

EAT 02Y B **Wipes face with napkin (not effective)**
Credit is given if the client picks up a napkin and
makes back-and-forth motions over mouth area. The
client need not effectively clean face, as long as an
attempt is made.

EAT 02Y C **Unwraps packaged food**
Credit is given if the client attempts to unwrap
various types of packaged food items with success on
more easily opened items such as candy and sticks
of gum. Use of teeth is permissable. The client
clearly demonstrates an understanding that the items

are edible but only after wrapping is removed. No physical assistance should be required.

EAT 02Y D   **Rejects inedible substances**
Credit is given if the client discriminates between edible and inedible substances. Inedible objects such as bones, rocks, or money are either not placed in the mouth or are rejected after being placed in mouth. No prompting should be necessary at this level.

EAT 02Y E   **Sets down glass with one hand or uses straw**
Credit is given if the client has accomplished *either* of the following two skills:

    1) Picks up glass, drinks and sets down without spilling and without assistance.

    2) Picks up and places straw in beverage and drinks through straw, with little spilling.

03 YEARS

EAT 03Y A   **Spears food with fork, carries food to mouth**
Credit is given if the client can independently feed self bite-size pieces of food with a fork and spears some items such as meat, string beans, etc., and does so with little spilling.

EAT 03Y B   **Carries spoon, without turning it, to mouth**
Credit is given if the client independently feeds self with spoon. As a result of effective manipulation of the spoon, little spilling occurs; and soft food is cut with spoon edge.

EAT 03Y C   **Eats meal without using fingers**
Credit is given if the client eats an entire meal using spoon or fork without using fingers to feed or push food onto utensil. Use of fingers is allowable with finger-appropriate foods such as bread, corn-on-the-cob, fried chicken, cookies, etc.

EAT 03Y D   **Gets drink without assistance**
Credit is given if the client independently obtains a drink by any two of the following three methods:

    1) Obtains and fills glass, turns tap on and off, and drinks without appreciable spilling (uses step stool or chair, if necessary).

    2) Pours beverage from manageable container into glass and drinks without appreciable spilling (fetches container and glass, if accessible).

3) Operates drinking fountain (uses step stool or chair, if necessary).

EAT 03Y E   **Holds cup by handle or pauses between sips**
Credit is given if the client demonstrates one of the following two skills:

1) Grasps a half-full cup of beverage with one hand, picks cup up and drinks contents with no appreciable spilling.

2) Pauses or sets down glass or cup between drinks or sips with no appreciable spilling.

04 YEARS

EAT 04Y A   **Cuts food with fork**
Credit is given if the client tears soft food such as hamburger and hot cakes with fork edge. This behavior should occur independently during meals.

EAT 04Y B   **Uses spoon and fork properly**
Credit is given if the client uses both spoon and fork discriminately during meal. The essence of this item is that given both utensils and a variety of foods, the client will use the fork with fork-appropriate foods, such as meats, and the spoon with spoon-appropriate foods, such as ice cream.

EAT 04Y C   **Tests food temperature and blows to cool**
Credit is given if the client tests hot food before placing in mouth and blows to cool. Persons at this level are aware of possible burns from eating hot food. Caution is exercised by testing the food with finger or sampling with small bites. Bites of hot food are blown on to cool.

EAT 04Y D   **Serves self "easy" foods with little spilling**
Credit is given if the client serves self "easy" foods from container with little spilling. Examples of easy foods include items such as mashed potatoes, oatmeal and cottage cheese. Persons at this level may require supervision as to choosing reasonable amounts of food.

EAT 04Y E   **Gets snack without assistance**
Credit is given if the client obtains a ready-to-eat snack from a storage area with permission, but without assistance. Opening of packages may be necessary. Ready-to-eat foods consist of such things

as fruit, cookies, potato chips, canned pop, etc. Storage areas consist of such things as refrigerator, cupboard, drawer, bowl, cookie jar, etc.

05 YEARS

EAT 05Y A   Cuts soft food with knife
Credit is given if the client cuts or slices soft food with a knife using a sawing motion. Soft foods consist of items such as soft cheese, loaf of bread, baked potato, fruit, meat loaf, baked dessert, etc. Persons at this level may require supervision when using a sharp knife.

EAT 05Y B   Spreads butter with knife
Credit is given if the client serves self bread or crackers and butter, jelly, cheese spread, peanut butter, etc., by spreading with a table or butter knife. Persons at this level should be able to prepare the above items without assistance and with little mess.

EAT 05Y C   Serves self "hard" foods with little spilling
Credit is given if the client serves self "hard" foods from container with little spilling. Examples of hard foods include items such as peaches, stew, soup, gravy, jello, etc. Persons at this level may require supervision as to choosing reasonable amounts of food.

EAT 05Y D   Obtains ingredients and prepares sandwich
Credit is given if the client independently obtains ingredients for and prepares a sandwich from at least three different food items. Given permission, persons at this level should be able to obtain ingredients from a variety of storage areas and prepare sandwiches made of reasonable combinations of items. Preparation skills required include unwrapping, spreading, slicing, cutting and layering of food items.

EAT 05Y E   Displays manners when directed
Credit is given if the client responds to directions such as, "chew with your mouth closed; don't eat with you fingers; don't talk with your mouth full; eat with your other hand in your lap; use your napkin"; etc.

08 YEARS

EAT 08Y A   **Cuts meat with knife and fork**

Credit is given if the client cuts food such as meat, with a knife and a fork. Persons at this level are able to immobilize meat such as tender steaks or roast, with a fork, while cutting bite-size portions with a knife, using a sawing motion. Assistance may be required for difficult steaks.

EAT 08Y B   **Uses can opener**

Credit is given if the client opens canned food with a can opener. Persons at this level can open small diameter (soup) cans with any one of the several standard-type openers available. Unfamiliar models may require a demonstration before successful use.

EAT 08Y C   **Chooses reasonable amounts of food**

Credit is given if the client serves self reasonable amounts from an assortment of several different types of food.

EAT 08Y D   **Prepares food (soup) following routine**

Credit is given if the client prepares simple foods following a learned routine. Persons at this level can mix and cook simple preparations such as fried or boiled eggs, soup, jello, grilled sandwiches, etc.

EAT 08Y E   **Displays manners when prompted**

Credit is given if the client displays acceptable manners when prompted. Examples of manners displayed at this level include using a napkin during meal, using utensils in an adult fashion, assuming correct eating posture, passing food correctly, engaging in appropriate table conversation, etc.

12 YEARS

EAT 12Y A   **Tests and seasons food to taste**

Credit is given if the client tastes food before adding seasoning and adjusts to suit taste. Persons at this level are able to judge reasonable amounts of seasoning to add to food.

EAT 12Y B   **Displays manners with few reminders**

Credit is given if the client displays acceptable manners and neatness without frequent reminders. Persons at this level are aware of rules of etiquette and require few reminders during meals in a family setting.

EAT 12Y C **Makes balanced meal using pictures of food**
Credit is given if the client constructs a balanced meal from an assortment of pictures or models of food. Persons at this level are aware of the four basic food groups and the importance of a balanced diet.

EAT 12Y D **Prepares food following recipes**
Credit is given if the client prepares foods following written recipes. Persons at this level are able to read recipes and prepare such items as cookies, cakes, hotcakes, etc.

EAT 12Y E **Considers cost when ordering from menu**
Credit is given if the client selects varied combinations from a short order menu. Persons at this level consider the cost of individual items and stay within the limits of money available for the total purchase.

16 YEARS

EAT 16Y A **Knows how to prevent and detect food spoilage**
Credit is given if the client demonstrates knowledge about detection and prevention of food spoilage. Persons at this level are able to answer questions about preventing spoilage through storage and preparation methods and are able to detect spoilage by changes in odor and consistency.

EAT 16Y B **Plans, buys, fixes, and serves adequate meal**
Credit is given if the client plans, purchases, prepares, and serves a complete and adequate meal for one or more persons.

EAT 16Y C **Knows simple nutrition facts**
Credit is given if the client demonstrates knowledge of simple nutrition facts. Persons at this level are able to answer nutritional questions concerning basic concepts such as balanced diet; daily caloric intake; vitamins and minerals; fat, carbohydrate and protein composition of foods; fiber v.s. processed foods; and weight control.

EAT 16Y D **Plans complete and adequate three-day menu**
Credit is given if the client plans complete, varied and adequate 3-day menu. Persons at this level are able to plan meals for a several day campout or vacation with family or peers.

EAT 16Y E **Considers cost, orders, and pays for meal out**
Credit is given if the client orders and pays for a
complete meal in a public restaurant with no
assistance.

TOILETING

03 MONTHS

TOI 03M A **Sits on toilet with considerable support**
Credit is given if the client sits on the toilet when supported. Persons at this level are able to sit in a special toileting chair when physically supported on the chair by another person.

TOI 03M B **Shows pattern for bowel movements**
Credit is given if the client exhibits some pattern in bowel movement when recorded over a 30-day period.

TOI 03M C **Eliminates occasionally if placed on toilet (BM)**
Credit is given if the client eliminates in the toilet when placed during the interval that bowel movement usually occurs. Persons at this level generally have a success rate of 10-25% when toileted according to a regular schedule.

06 MONTHS

TOI 06M A **Sits on toilet with little support**
Credit is given if the client is able to sit in a special toileting chair which is equipped with supportive devices. Persons at this level do not require physical assistance other than help in getting on and off of the chair or help in remaining seated. A seat belt is sometimes used for protection and as an aid to keep the person seated.

TOI 06M B **Remains dry for one hour**
Credit is given if the client's elimination chart indicates intervals of dryness from one to two hours in length.

TOI 06M C **Eliminates at end of a dry period if toileted**
Credit is given if the client eliminates in the toilet when placed at the time when urination usually occurs. Persons at this level generally have a 10-25% success rate when toileted according to a regular schedule.

12 MONTHS

TOI 12M A **Sits on toilet when left alone**
Credit is given if the client remains seated on a toilet when left alone. Persons at this level are able to sit on an appropriately sized toilet seat for five minutes without assistance. Help may be required in getting on and off the toilet but mechanical or physical assistance is not required for support, or to keep the person seated for short periods.

TOI 12M B **Wakes up dry from sleep**
Credit is given if the client awakens dry from nap or sleep. Persons at this level generally awaken dry 10-25% of the time.

TOI 12M C **Urinates after awakening**
Credit is given if the client urinates in the toilet after awakening. Persons at this level generally urinate soon after awakening. If toileted at this time, a success rate of 25-50% may be achieved.

TOI 12M D **Eliminates if toileted at customary time (BM)**
Credit is given if the client eliminates in the toilet when placed during the interval that bowel movement usually occurs. Persons at this level generally have a success rate of 25-50% when toileted according to a regular interval.

TOI 12M E **Shows signs of discomfort when wet or soiled**
Credit is given if the client exhibits signs of discomfort when wet or soiled. Persons at this level may complain by fussing or crying until changed.

18 MONTHS

TOI 18M A **Stays dry most of day when toileted**
Credit is given if the client has few daytime accidents when toileted on a regular basis. Persons at this level generally have a success rate of 50-75% when toileted periodically throughout the day.

TOI 18M B **Reports accidents by word, sound, etc.**
Credit is given if the client indicates that an accident has occurred by word, sound or gesture. Persons at this level may communicate in a variety of ways, including pointing to or pulling at pants, bringing fresh clothing, and saying toileting words such as "potty"

TOI 18M C **Goes into bathroom when directed**
Credit is given if the client goes into the bathroom area when told to do so. Persons at this level may be inconsistent in responding to verbal directions, but generally respond at least half of the time.

TOI 18M D **Requests toilet by word or gesture**
Credit is given if the client occasionally requests, in some manner, need for toilet. Persons at this level generally use one word or gesture for indicating both types of toilet functions.

TOI 18M E **Responds to question as to need for toilet**
Credit is given if the client responds to questions such as, "Do you have to go potty?" Persons at this level communicate with responses such as nodding head, saying no, or heading for the bathroom.

02 YEARS

TOI 02Y A **Verbalizes or gestures toilet need**
Credit is given if the client usually requests, in some manner, need for toilet. Persons at this level generally use two different words or gestures for distinguishing between bowel and bladder functions.

TOI 02Y B **Places self on toilet when directed**
Credit is given if the client sits on the toilet when verbally directed. Persons at this level may need help pulling down pants, but are able to position themselves on an appropriately sized toilet. Few accidents should occur if the client is regularly toileted.

TOI 02Y C **Indicates when finished on toilet**
Credit is given if the client indicates when finished on the toilet by actions such as calling, standing up, attempting to pull pants up, or walking out of bathroom.

TOI 02Y D **Takes off wet pants**
Credit is given if the client removes wet or soiled clothing on own initiative or when verbally directed. Persons at this level will try to remove wet or soiled clothing but may require assistance when wearing shoes.

TOI 02Y E **Pushes down own pants when toileted**
Credit is given if the client pushes down pants during toileting when verbally prompted. Persons at this level may occasionally push down their pants unprompted.

03 YEARS

TOI 03Y A Places self on toilet alone
Credit is given if the client usually places self on the toilet without prompting. Persons at this level require occasional reminders but are able to self-initiate toileting without reminders at least half of the time. Few accidents should occur at this level.

TOI 03Y B Wipes self when told
Credit is given if the client wipes self when verbally prompted. Persons at this level are not very effective at wiping, but do make an attempt when given toilet paper and told to wipe. Assistance may be required for completing the job adequately.

TOI 03Y C Flushes toilet alone
Credit is given if the client flushes the toilet after use, on own initiative. Persons at this level require frequent reminders, but do flush the toilet without prompting, at least some of the time.

TOI 03Y D Remains dry at night when routinely awakened
Credit is given if the client remains dry at night when routinely awakened. Persons at this level should have few nighttime accidents when toileted during the night.

TOI 03Y E Manages own clothing in toileting situation with help
Credit is given if the client manages own clothing in a toileting situation with little assistance. Persons at this level are able to push down and pull up pants and underpants without help and do so on their own initiative. Help is generally required with fasteners.

04 YEARS

TOI 04Y A Uses toilet on own initiative
Credit is given if the client takes responsibility for own toileting needs in the home. Persons at this level have no daytime accidents under normal circumstances when a familiar bathroom is readily available.

TOI 04Y B Wipes self with reminders
Credit is given if the client wipes self when prompted or on own initiative. Persons at this level sometime wipe themselves without prompting, but are not consistent. Frequent reminding and checking is required.

TOI 04Y C **Remains dry at night**
Credit is given if the client remains dry at night without being routinely awakened. Persons at this level may have some nighttime accidents, but awaken dry more than half of the time.

TOI 04Y D **Washes hands after toileting when verbally prompted**
Credit is given if the client washes and dries hands after toileting. Persons at this level wash and dry their hands effectively after toileting but require frequent reminders.

TOI 04Y E **Manages own clothing in toileting situation without help**
Credit is given if the client manages own clothing in a toileting situation without assistance. Persons at this level are able to push down and pull up pants and underpants without help and do so on their own initiative. Help is only required for difficult fasteners.

05 YEARS

TOI 05Y A **Handles toileting in strange setting with aid**
Credit is given if the client handles own toileting in unfamiliar surroundings when accompanied by an adult. Persons at this level are able to toilet self independently, but may require reminders to insure that proper hygiene practices are observed.

TOI 05Y B **Wipes self adequately**
Credit is given if the client wipes self without reminders. Persons at this level usually clean themselves adequately when they wipe, but occasional reminders may be required as evidenced by stains on underpants.

TOI 05Y C **Flushes toilet on own initiative**
Credit is given if the client flushes the toilet after use without reminders. Persons at this level usually flush the toilet on own initiative; however, occasional reminders may be required.

TOI 05Y D **Washes hands after toileting**
Credit is given if the client washes hands after toileting without reminders. Persons at this level generally wash their hands after toileting, especially in public restrooms. Occasional reminders may still be required.

TOI 05Y E   **Adjusts clothing before leaving lavatory**
Credit is given if the client's appearance is present-able when leaving lavatory after toileting. Persons at this level may require occasional reminders to zip pants, buckle belt or tuck in shirt; but generally these tasks are performed independently.

08 YEARS

TOI 08Y A   **Uses toilet before going out**
Credit is given if the client uses the toilet before go-ing out or on a trip. Persons at this level may require occasional reminders, but generally this activity is performed independently.

TOI 08Y B   **Distinguishes sex identification signs**
Credit is given if the client defferentiates between the signs and symbols used to identify men's and women's restrooms in public places. Persons at this level are able to read or recognize common signs and symbols such as men/women, ladies/gentlemen, boys/girls, and international symbols.

TOI 08Y C   **Closes door while using toilet**
Credit is given if the client closes the restroom door when using the toilet. Persons at this level seldom need reminding in this regard.

TOI 08Y D   **Uses toilet seat protector when reminded**
Credit is given if the client uses toilet seat protectors in public restrooms. Persons at this level require reminders, but do not require assistance in the actual use of the protector.

TOI 08Y E   **Uses soap and towel dispensers**
Credit is given if the client uses soap and towel dispensers or wall-mounted blow dryers, in public restrooms. Persons at this level may need to be in-structed in the operation of unfamiliar devices, but do not require assistance with devices after exposure.

12 YEARS

TOI 12Y A   **Locates restroom in unfamiliar places**
Credit is given if the client locates restrooms in a variety of unfamiliar settings. Persons at this level are able to locate restrooms in public places when alone or unsupervised by an adult. Locating methods in-

clude asking store clerks, using a store directory, and searching in likely locations.

TOI 12Y B **Uses locks and latches to insure privacy**
Credit is given if the client routinely locks the door of bathrooms, restrooms, or privacy stalls, when other people are present.

TOI 12Y C **Cleans up after self before leaving bathroom in home**
Credit is given if the client tidies up before leaving the bathroom in their own home. Persons at this level may require reminders, but routinely practice learned social conventions such as lowering or wiping off the seat, returning soap to the dish, and wiping off the counter.

TOI 12Y D **Uses bathroom correctly when visiting**
Credit is given if the client uses bathroom facilities appropriately when visiting. Persons at this level may need to be reminded of proper guest behavior prior to the visit, but once reminded, they are able to observe proprieties such as only using items reserved for guests, washing out the sink after use, using air fresheners, refraining from going through drawers and cupboards, and generally leaving the bathroom in the same condition found prior to their use.

TOI 12Y E **Uses toilet seat protector independently**
Credit is given if the client routinely uses paper toilet seat protectors in public restrooms. Persons at this level do not require repeated prompts, once instructed.

16 YEARS
TOI 16Y A **Explains the importance of regularity**
Credit is given if the client describes the importance of regular bowel and urine eliminations. Persons at this level should be able to convey at least a basic idea that elimination rids the body of digestive wastes which, if retained, could cause ill health.

TOI 16Y B **Understands common treatments of irregularity**
Credit is given if the client describes several methods for treating irregularity and the advantages of each. Persons at this level should be able to name treatment methods such as enemas, suppositories, oral

laxatives, eating certain types of fruit, increasing fiber intake, eating cereals, and eating foods containing bran.

TOI 16Y C **Describes symptoms of serious elimination problems**

Credit is given if the client is able to describe some of the symptoms of elimination problems which require consultation with a knowledgeable person or physician. Persons at this level should have a basic understanding of the seriousness of problems such as prolonged constipation, bloody stool, prolonged diarrhea, painful urination, or blood in the urine.

TOI 16Y D **Explains unusual toileting circumstances**

Credit is given if the client describes the toileting methods to be used in a variety of unusual circumstances. Persons at this level are able to describe courses of action they might take in situations such as camping in the woods, social stiuations where leaving is difficult, riding in a car, using the public transportation system, and finding that toilet paper is unavailable.

TOI 16Y E **Demonstrates methods for correcting malfunctioning toilet**

Credit is given if the client demonstrates or describes methods for handling toilet malfunctions. Persons at this level should be able to demonstrate or describe methods such as unstopping a plugged toilet with a plunger, stopping an overflowing toilet by turning off the water or lifting the float, or flushing a toilet by pouring water into it.

DRESSING

03 MONTHS

DRE 03M A Manipulates bedcover with hands
Credit is given if the client randomly fingers, grasps, or pulls sheets or blankets on the bed. The manual exploration at this level is important in the development of environmental awareness of cloth and coverings.

DRE 03M B Manipulates own clothing with hands
Credit is given if the client randomly explores own clothing by fingering, grasping, or pulling with hands. The manual exploration at this level is important in the development of the environmental awareness of cloth and other material used as body coverings.

DRE 03M C Anticipates dressing and undressing
Credit is given if the client exhibits signs of anticipating being dressed or undressed. Persons at this level exhibit anticipatory signs such as increasing activity, opening eyes wider, or becoming still.

06 MONTHS

DRE 06M A Removes foot coverings
Credit is given if the client is able to remove loosely fitting slippers, shoes, or stockings. Persons at this level are able to intentionally remove foot coverings but don't necessarily do so as an act of undressing or when prompted, but rather as a game or novel activity which is rewarding in itself.

DRE 06M B Manipulates discrete parts of clothing
Credit is given if the client handles and feels discrete parts of clothing such as buttons and shoestrings. Persons at this level exhibit increased discrimination of clothing as evidenced by manipulations of specific clothing parts.

DRE 06Y C Cooperates actively when dressed and undressed
Credit is given if the client actively cooperates during dressing and undressing routines. Persons at this

level may learn to resist being dressed and undressed unless the activity is rewarded through pleasurable social interactions and games. Active cooperation is typically accomplished through dressing games such as playing peek-a-boo with pullover garments.

12 Months

DRE 12M A **Removes socks or untied shoes**

Credit is given if the client removes socks or untied shoes. Persons at this level remove foot coverings intentionally and as an act of undressing. This behavior does not necessarily occur when the person is directed to remove the article, but occurs unprompted as the result of imitation.

DRE 12M B **Pulls off pants**

Credit is given if the client occasionaly pulls off pants. Persons at this level are behaving in a purposeful manner as a result of imitation but do not necessarily remove pants at the appropriate time or as a result of verbal prompting.

DRE 12M C **Directs arm into armhole**

Credit is given if the client directs arm into armhole of garment when being dressed. When presented with a coat or shirt positioned to receive the arm, persons at this level respond by extending the arm toward or into the sleeve.

DRE 12M D **Extends leg to have pants put on**

Credit is given if the client raises or extends leg when presented with pants during dressing routines. Persons at this level exhibit this behavior at the sight of the pants or when the pants are positioned on the foot.

DRE 12M E **Imitates putting on hat**

Credit is given if the client puts hat on head unprompted, or as the result of imitation. Persons at this level are able to intentionally place a hat on their head but may do so as an act of play rather than an act of dressing for the out-of-doors. The position or alignment of the hat on the head in not important for crediting this item.

18 MONTHS

DRE 18M A Directs toe into shoe
Credit is given if the client tries to put on shoes. Persons at this level are usually only able to sucessfully put on shoes that are much larger than their feet. But they do try to put on their shoes, especially when a shoe has fallen off or when they are being dressed.

DRE 18M B Removes unbuttoned jacket or shirt
Credit is given if the client removes loosely fitting, un-buttoned jacket or shirt when verbally prompted. Persons at this level do not need physical assistance except with difficult garments.

DRE 18M C Takes off mittens or gloves
Credit is given if the client removes mittens or gloves when verbally prompted. Persons at this level do not require physical assistance under ordinary circumstances.

DRE 18M D Directs leg into pant leg
Credit is given if the client is able to guide foot into pant leg that is held in position by another person. Persons at this level are able to aim their foot and push it into the pant leg. They do this when prompted by the sight of the pants or when verbally directed.

DRE 18M E Unzips easy zipper
Credit is given if the client is able to unzip zippers that work easily and have easy-to-grasp clasps. Persons at this level are able to manage some coat zippers, but usually have difficulty with zippers on pants.

02 YEARS

DRE 02Y A Removes untied shoes when verbally prompted
Credit is given if the client is able to remove untied shoes when verbally directed to do so. Persons at this level are not able to untie shoes but can remove untied or loosely fitting shoes or slippers and do so as an act of undressing.

DRE 02Y B Pushes down pants when verbally prompted
Credit is given if the client pushes down pants when verbally directed to do so. Persons at this level, generally, are unable to loosen fasteners, but are able to lower unfastened or loosely fitting pants as an act of undressing or during toileting.

DRE 02Y C Pulls up pants once started
Credit is given if the client finishes pulling up pants that have already been pulled up over the feet. Persons at this level are not able to pull pants over feet, but are able to complete pulling up pants and do so as an act of dressing. This behavior occurs when the client is verbally prompted or spontaneously as a result of increased awareness and anticipation of dressing routines.

DRE 02Y D Attempts to put on pants without help
Credit is given if the client tries to put on pants without help but usually is unsuccessful. Often, both feet are placed in the same pant leg. Persons at this level respond to verbal prompting but also may try to put on pants spontaneously.

DRE 02Y E Finds armholes and thrusts arms into them
Credit is given if the client puts one arm into the armhole of a garment which is positioned by the arm. Persons at this level are able to get their first arm into the armhole held before them, but may need assistance with the second armhole. This behavior occurs when the client is verbally prompted, but usually the sight of the garment is prompt enough.

03 YEARS

DRE 03Y A Tries to put on shoes and socks
Credit is given if the client successfully puts on shoes and socks but not necessarily in the proper manner. Persons at this level often put shoes on the wrong feet and place socks on their feet with the heels in an incorrect position. They are able to switch shoes when informed of the error, but physical assistance is usually required for re-positioning of socks.

DRE 03Y B Undresses with help on fasteners only
Credit is given if the client independently removes clothing as part of an undressing routine. Persons at this level undress themselves without help except for difficult fasteners such as snaps, belts, zippers, buttons and knots.

DRE 03Y C Dresses self in wardrobe already laid out
Credit is given if the client is able to dress self in a simple wardrobe which is placed on a chair or bed.

Persons at this level are able to perform this task independently, but may require physical assistance with difficult fasteners. This item is credited even if articles are put on backwards or inside-out; however, the client should be able to make the necessary corrections when verbally prompted.

DRE 03Y D **Fetches clothing article from storage**
Credit is given if the client follows simple requests to bring back single clothing items from storage areas. Persons at this level are able to carry out requests such as, "go get your socks out of your drawer."

DRE 03Y E **Unbuttons front buttons**
Credit is given if the client unbuttons front buttons independently as an act of undressing. Persons at this level recognize that unbuttoning is necessary for certain types of clothing to be removed and will unbutton automatically when told to undress or take off their shirt.

04 YEARS

DRE 04Y A **Puts on socks with heels down**
Credit is given if the client puts on socks with heels down. Persons at this level require no assistance as long as socks are loose enough to be easily managed.

DRE 04Y B **Distinguishes front from back of garments**
Credit is given if the client puts on most garments with the correct front/back position. Persons at this level are able to distinguish the front and back of garments most of the time.

DRE 04Y C **Dresses self with little assistance**
Credit is given if the client is able to dress with little assistance. Persons at this level are able to locate and put on basic articles of clothing. No assistance should be required except with difficult fasteners and tying shoes.

DRE 04Y D **Laces shoes**
Credit is given if the client laces own shoes without assistance. Persons at this level are able to lace shoes but may have problems getting both string ends even.

DRE 04Y E **Buttons front buttons**
Credit is given if the client buttons front buttons without assistance. Persons at this level are able to fasten front buttons but may still require reminders regarding lining up buttons with respective holes.

05 YEARS

DRE 05Y A **Puts shoes on correct feet**
Credit is given if the client puts on shoes and consistently gets them on the correct feet without assistance. Persons at this level should have no problems unless the shoes are unusually shaped.

DRE 05Y B **Turns slipover garment right-side-out**
Credit is given if the client is able to correct pullover garments which are inside-out. Persons at this level may not always dress self with garments right-side-out, but when errors are brought to their attention, they are able to correct the matter without further assistance.

DRE 05Y C **Places clothes in appropriate drawers**
Credit is given if the client places basic articles of clothing in appropriate drawers unassisted. Persons at this level are able to store basic items such as T-shirts, underpants, and socks. Typically, clients perform this task when handed an assorted stack of clothing and are instructed to place the clothing in the drawers.

DRE 05Y D **Unties loose knots**
Credit is given if the client unties loose knots in clothing items such as scarves and shoelaces. Persons at this level are able to untie loose knots when verbally prompted and commonly do so unprompted during dressing and undressing routines.

DRE 05Y E **Buckles and unbuckles belts, shoes or galoshes**
Credit is given if the client fastens and unfastens buckles on garments. Persons at this level can operate buckles such as those on belts and are able to do so without assistance.

08 YEARS

DRE 08Y A **Changes clothes as required by routine**
Credit is given if the client changes clothing regularly according to a learned required routine. Persons at

this level require occasional reminders, but typically observe rules such as changing to play clothing when returning from school.

DRE 08Y B Helps select new clothes
Credit is given if the client actively participates in the selection of clothing purchases at stores. Persons at this level express distinct preferences between items but still require assistance with fit and coordination.

DRE 08Y C Selects clothing suitable to weather
Credit is given if the client selects out-of-door clothing suitable to the weather. Persons at this level dress in weather appropriate clothing when leaving their place of residence, and they usually do so without need for reminders or prompting.

DRE 08Y D Keeps shoelaces tied without reminder
Credit is given if the client keeps shoelaces tied without need for reminders or prompting. Persons at this level are able to tie shoes without assistance and keep them tied as a matter of routine.

DRE 08Y E Zips jacket zippers without help
Credit is given if the client zips jacket zippers without assistance. Persons at this level may require occasional reminders to zip their jacket when outside during cold weather, but they are able to zip unassisted and usually do so when the need arises.

12 YEARS
DRE 12Y A Shines shoes or washes socks
Credit is given if the client demonstrates rudimentary skills in clothing care and maintenance. Persons at this level are able to perform tasks such as shining shoes and washing or rinsing socks or nylons. Typically, however, reminding or prompting is required for the person to engage in these activities unless the activities have been incorporated into their habitual routine.

DRE 12Y B Picks new clothes with advice
Credit is given if the client shops for and picks out new clothes with little need for assistance. Persons at this level are able to shop for clothing and make purchases within the money allowance they have in their possession, but they do need advice prior to the pur-

chases with regard to size, style, and coordination with other wardrobe items. Typically, clothing purchases are made when they are accompanied by an adult, however these persons are able to perform this activity when alone or accompanied by a peer.

DRE 12Y C Selects garments appropriate to occasion
Credit is given if the client is able to independently select clothing from a wardrobe suitable for a variety of occasions. Persons at this level are able to dress appropriately for occasions such as attending church, going out to a nice restaurant, or engaging in work or play. Typically, this skill is performed independently once the client is notified of the forthcoming event.

DRE 12Y D Tries on clothes before buying
Credit is given if the client judges the fit of garments before making a purchase. Persons at this level are able to try on clothing before buying and make reasonable judgements as to appropriateness of fit.

DRE 12Y E Hangs clothes up on hangers
Credit is given if the client arranges clothing in appropriate manner on hangers and places on closet rod for storage. Persons at this level are able to hang up items such as pants, shirts, dresses, and coats and are able to button top button of shirts, etc., so that the items stay on hangers.

16 YEARS

DRE 16Y A Washes, dries, and irons clothing
Credit is given if the client washes and properly dries or irons garments without assistance. Persons at this level are able to operate electric washers and dryers and also are able to hang up clothes to dry on line or rack.

DRE 16Y B Budgets for and buys wardrobe
Credit is given if the client budgets for and purchases day-to-day wardrobe. Persons at this level are able to budget an allowance or other income and assume responsiblility for maintaining and augmenting personal wardrobe.

DRE 16Y C Prepares list of needed clothing
Credit is given if the client prepares a list of needed clothing articles upon request or in preparation for a

shopping trip. Persons at this level are able to analyze needs and prepare lists including correct size and wanted colors and styles.

DRE 16Y D **Performs simple mending**
Credit is given if the client is able to perform simple mending of clothing without assistance. Persons at this level are able to perform mending tasks such as replacing buttons, sewing on straps, or applying patches.

DRE 16Y E **Maintains orderly clothing area**
Credit is given if the client usually maintains an orderly clothing area. Persons at this level are able to make their clothing areas look good when adequately motivated to do so. Verbal correction may occasionally be necessary to maintain acceptable standards of neatness.

HEALTH & GROOMING

03 MONTHS

H&G 03M A **Lies in shallow bath, partly supports head**
Credit is given if the client partially supports own head when lying on stomach or back in shallow bath. Persons at this level are able to lift head and hold in mid-position for short periods when on back or stomach. Typically, the trainer's hand is held under the head to protect against the possibility of the face becoming submerged. Considerable support is necessary for safety, but complete support is not required.

H&G 03M B **Sits in bath when supported**
Credit is given if the client helps to maintain sitting position in bath. Persons at this level are able to sit supported, and hold their head erect with little head bobbing. Typically, the trainer provides support by holding his or her hand against the back of the client.

H&G 03M C **Cooperates while in bath**
Credit is given if the client cooperates during bathing procedures. Persons at this level generally enjoy baths as evidenced by responses such as becoming quiet, laughing or splashing.

H&G 03M D **Closes eyes when face is washed**
Credit is given if the client closes eyes when face is washed with a washcloth.

H&G 03M E **Grasps washcloth placed in hand**
Credit is given if the client grasps washcloth placed in hand, and retains washcloth in grasp for brief period.

06 MONTHS

H&G 06M A **Sits in bath with little support**
Credit is given if the client sits unsupported in shallow bath. Persons at this level are able to sit steadily with little or no support for several minutes.

H&G 06M B Closes eyes when approached by washcloth
Credit is given if the client closes eyes when face is approached with a washcloth held by another. Persons at this level anticipate having their face washed as evidenced by their turning their face away from an approaching washcloth or by closing their eyes.

H&G 06M C Grasps washcloth within reach
Credit is given if the client picks up washcloth that is placed within reach. Persons at this level will do this spontaneously as an expression of curiosity and as an act of exploration. To elicit this behavior by prompting requires that the trainer employ physical assistance in placing the client's hand on the washcloth.

H&G 06M D Lies in shallow bath, completely supports head
Credit is given if the client completely supports own head when lying on stomach or back in a shallow bath. Persons at this level have good head control and are able to maintain control for prolonged periods. Typically, the trainer's hand is held under the head to protect against accidental submersion of the face.

12 MONTHS

H&G 12M A Places hands in water when assisted
Credit is given if the client places hands in water in response to gestural prompting. Persons at this level will place their hands in warm water in imitation (after being shown or physically assisted by having their hands placed in the water).

H&G 12M B Touches face with washcloth when assisted
Credit is given if the client touches face with washcloth in response to gestural prompting. Persons at this level are able to perform this behavior in imitation after seeing it done by another, or after having the washcloth placed in the hand and being physically assisted in touching it to the face.

H&G 12M C Puts soap on soapdish when assisted
Credit is given if the client returns soap to proper location in response to gestural prompting. Persons at this level are able to return soap to locations such as soapdish or side of sink after being shown how or after being physically assisted.

H&G 12M D Touches head with comb when assisted
Credit is given if the client touches head with comb in response to gestural prompting. Persons at this level are able to perform this behavior in imitation after being shown how or after being physically assisted.

H&G 12M E Puts toothbrush in mouth when assisted
Credit is given if the client places toothbrush in mouth in response to gestural prompting. Persons at this level are able to perform this behavior in imitation after being shown how or after being physically assisted.

18 MONTHS

H&G 18M A Makes handwashing motion when requested
Credit is given if the client attempts to wash hands in response to verbal prompting. Persons at this level typically place hands in water and rub hands together when told to do so. Washing attempts are ineffectual but clearly demonstrate an awareness of the intent of the command.

H&G 18M B Wipes face with washcloth when requested
Credit is given if the client attempts to wash face with washcloth when verbally prompted. Persons at this level are able to wipe their face with a washcloth when told to do so. Washing attempts are ineffectual but clearly demonstrate an awareness of the intent of the command.

H&G 18M C Blows nose when hanky is held to it
Credit is given if the client blows nose when handkerchief or tissue is held to it by the trainer and a verbal request is made to blow.

H&G 18M D Picks up comb and "combs" hair upon request
Credit is given if the client picks up comb or brush and makes combing movements when verbally requested. Persons at this level are able to make combing movements but may not always direct the teeth or bristles toward the hair.

H&G 18M E Applies soap to hands
Credit is given if the client applies some soap to hands. Persons at this level are not able to produce lather but are able to get some soap on hands by means such as patting or rubbing and do so in response to verbal prompting.

02 YEARS

H&G 02Y A Tries to wash hands with soap and water
Credit is given if the client is able to wash own hands with soap and water. Persons at this level are able to turn on water, get soap and water on their hands, and rub their hands together. Typically, washing attempts are not effective; and hands may not be thoroughly rinsed.

H&G 02Y B Tries to dry hands
Credit is given if the client tries to dry own hands. Persons at this level are able to pick up the towel and make an attempt at drying. Awareness of drying intent is clearly demonstrated, but efforts are not very effective.

H&G 02Y C Comes when called for health and grooming activities
Credit is given if the client comes when called for health, hygiene, or grooming activities. Persons at this level come when called and learn to come consistently for routines that are made pleasurable. For example, the client will come consistently for routine medication if the medication is paired with an edible treat.

H&G 02Y D Applies soap to body parts
Credit is given if the client applies soap to various parts of the body when given directions. Persons at this level are able to apply soap to some named body areas but require considerable gestural assistance to attain any degree of adequate soap coverage. Typical responses to directions involve applying soap to convenient small areas on the named body part.

H&G 02Y E Puts toothbrush in mouth and "brushes"
Credit is given if the client puts toothbrush in mouth and makes brushing movements. Persons at this level are ineffective but are able to demonstrate awareness of the task by clearly trying to brush.

03 YEARS

H&G 03Y A Indicates when sick or injured
Credit is given if the client indicates when fatigued, sick or injured. Persons at this level are able to communicate these physical needs by methods such as

pointing to an injured body part or making statements such as "hurt" or "I go to bed".

H&G 03Y B Dries own hands effectively

Credit is given if the client is able to dry own hands effectively. Persons at this level may need occasional verbal reminders to dry after washing, but they are able to get their hands reasonably dry without additional assistance.

H&G 03Y C Blows and wipes nose when reminded

Credit is given if the client blows and wipes own nose when reminded. Persons at this level will attempt to blow and wipe own nose when handed a handkerchief or tissue and told to wipe or blow. Cleaning attempts are not very effective, and frequent checking and reminders may be required when nasal discharge is especially prevalent.

H&G 03Y D Avoids hazards or dangers

Credit is given if the client avoids common health hazards or dangers. Persons at this level typically have learned to avoid common everyday hazards or dangers such as slippery floors, moving vehicles or objects, broken glass, hot stoves, etc.

H&G 03Y E Puts toothpaste on toothbrush

Credit is given if the client applies toothpaste to a toothbrush. Persons at this level are able to remove the cap from the toothpaste tube and squeeze the paste onto the bristles. Performance of this skill typically requires verbal prompting and is often included as part of a larger toothbrushing sequence. Close supervision may be required to prevent messes and insure that the cap is replaced on the tube.

04 YEARS

H&G 04Y A Washes hands effectively

Credit is given if the client is able to wash own hands with soap and water. Persons at this level are able to turn on the water, get soap and water on their hands, and rub their hands together. Typically, washing attempts are effective (towel is not soiled when hands are dried), and hands are thoroughly rinsed. Attempts may be made to adjust water temperature, but assistance is still required for proper adjustment.

H&G 04Y B Dries most of self
Credit is given if the client dries most of self as part of a bathing routine. Persons at this level may miss hard-to-reach parts such as the back, but typically are able to dry themselves reasonably well with very little assistance.

H&G 04Y C Washes self effectively
Credit is given if the client washes self effectively with verbal directions. Persons at this level are able to get themselves reasonably clean if closely supervised and given part-by-part suggestions as to what needs to be washed.

H&G 04Y D Avoids eating food dropped on floor
Credit is given if the client avoids eating food dropped on the floor. Persons at this level still require assistance in discriminating between situations when food may or may not be consumed after being dropped. However, food dropped is not indiscriminately eaten without inspection, cleaning or consultation with another person.

H&G 04Y E Brushes teeth with directions
Credit is given if the client tries to brush own teeth and is able to cover most surface areas if given step-by-step instructions and demonstration. Persons at this level may have difficulty with proper angles and motions, but are able to respond to directions such as "brush back and forth" and "brush up and down".

05 YEARS

H&G 05Y A Localizes site of discomfort
Credit is given if the client is able to indicate the site of discomfort on the body. Persons at this level are able to indicate when they are sick or hurt and are able to tell where they hurt by either pointing to, touching, or naming the affected body part.

H&G 05Y B Bathes self when supervised
Credit is given if the client bathes self when told to take a bath. Persons at this level are able to go through all of the motions of bathing but require supervision in the form of checking and touching up to insure an adequate and thorough job.

H&G 05Y C Keeps nose clean

Credit is given if the client blows and wipes own nose without assistance. Persons at this level are able to wipe and blow their own nose and usually do so without reminders.

H&G 05Y D Combs hair so it falls in one direction

Credit is given if the client combs or brushes own hair so it lies in one direction. Persons at this level typically have problems making a part in hair but can use a comb or brush to smooth the hair so it falls in one direction.

H&G 05Y E Adjusts water temperature

Credit is given if the client adjusts water temperature at sink or tub. Persons at this level do not require assistance with familiar types of faucets, but may need assistance with unfamiliar faucets or out-of-reach faucets in shower stalls. Water temperature is typically tested with finger, hand, or foot employing trial-and-error testing and adjustment. Caution is observed before commiting entire body or part of body to the water.

08 YEARS

H&G 08Y A Treats minor illness or injury

Credit is given if the client demonstrates ability to seek advice and follow instructions regarding simple treatments for minor health problems. Persons at this level are able to carryout treatments such as washing a scrape with soap and water, treating a cut with antiseptic and a band-aid, applying a compress to a nosebleed, placing a burned finger in cold water, taking aspirin for headache or fever or taking a single medication following a schedule.

H&G 08Y B Performs complete bathing sequence

Credit is given if the client bathes self completely without assistance. Persons at this level are able to start the water, adjust temperature, clean themselves effectively and dry themselves without assistance. Verbal prompting may occasionally be necessary to get the client started, but actual assistance is not required.

H&G 08Y C Cuts own fingernails
Credit is given if the client is able to trim own fingernails using nail clippers or scissors. Persons at this level are able to trim nails and can do so with caution after training and counseling as to hazards. Assistance may be needed when trimming the dominant hand.

H&G 08Y D Shampoos and combs hair adequately
Credit is given if the client shampoos and grooms own hair without assistance. Persons at this level are able to completely shampoo their own hair and perform simple grooming tasks such as brushing or combing, parting, and blow drying.

H&G 08Y E Brushes own teeth
Credit is given if the client performs a complete sequence for brushing teeth correctly. Persons at this level are able to brush own teeth satisfactorily (brush all surfaces) if properly motivated, but checking may still be required to insure consistency.

12 YEARS

H&G 12Y A Takes own medication for short intervals
Credit is given if the client controls and dispenses own medication to self for short periods. Persons at this level are able to take complete responsibility for own medication if checked periodically (e.g., at the end of each day, etc.).

H&G 12Y B Recognizes symptoms of illness
Credit is given if the client demonstrates knowledge of the common symptoms of ill health. Persons at this level know when they are sick, have a good idea of what common illness they probably have, and initiate or seek appropriate treatments. They are able to correctly answer questions such as what to do for a burn, open wound, nausea, nosebleed and fever.

H&G 12Y C Maintains body cleanliness
Credit is given if the client maintains satisfactory body cleanliness with little reminding. Persons at this level are able to perform all of their hygiene requirements without assistance except for occasional checking. Typical hygiene activities include routine bathing, shaving, use of sanitary napkins, care of nails and use of deodorant.

H&G 12Y D **Maintains satisfactory dental hygiene**
Credit is given if the client maintains satisfactory dental hygiene without assistance. Persons at this level are able to brush their teeth routinely with little need for checking. Routine dental care also may include the use of dental floss and mouthwash.

H&G 12Y E **Answers simple questions about reproduction**
Credit is given if the client demonstrates rudimentary knowledge of simple reproduction facts. Persons at this level are able to answer questions and convey awareness of concepts such as length of pregnancy, basic anatomy of reproduction, egg, sperm, womb, and menstruation.

16 YEARS

H&G 16Y A **Takes responsibility for own medications**
Credit is given if the client takes complete responsibility for own medication. Persons at this level are able to get a prescription filled, store the medication appropriately and take the medication following written instructions.

H&G 16Y B **Arranges and reports for medical appointments**
Credit is given if the client takes an active role in deciding when medical and dental appointments should be made and takes complete responsibility for reporting at the appointed time.

H&G 16Y C **Answers basic questions about first aid**
Credit is given if the client demonstrates useful knowledge about basic first aid facts. Persons at this level can describe appropriate actions in emergencies resulting in burns, poisoning, drowning, shock, bleeding and broken bones.

H&G 16Y D **Maintains acceptable appearance**
Credit is given if the client maintains acceptable appearance, and cleanliness without assistance. Persons at this level are able to take complete responsibility for appearance including make-up, hairdo, clothing and hygiene.

H&G 16Y E Answers questions about VD and pregnancy prevention

Credit is given if the client demonstrates knowledge regarding the cause and prevention of VD and pregnancy. Persons at this level are aware of facts such as responsibility related to pregnancy, symptoms of VD and methods of VD protection and birth control.

COMMUNICATION

03 MONTHS
COM 03M A **Attends to environmental sounds**
Credit is given if the client attends briefly to environmental sounds. Persons at this level notice and attend to sounds, especially the human voice. Typical responses include looking at or in direction of object being tapped, quieting and listening to voices or music, and searching with eyes for a sound.

COM 03M B **Attends to environmental sights**
Credit is given if the client attends briefly to environmental sights. Persons at this level follow moving objects with eyes and attend briefly to novel objects such as a toy, picture, or projected image such as TV or movie.

COM 03M C **Vocalizes two different sounds**
Credit is given if the client vocalizes two different distinct sounds or syllables other than those used when crying or fussing. Persons at this level are able to vocalize simple sounds, especially vowel-like sounds such as ooh, ah, ae, eh and uh.

COM 03M D **Communicates basic needs**
Credit is given if the client communicates basic needs or attitudes through vocalizations or facial expressions. Persons at this level whimper or cry when hungry or uncomfortable and smile or vocalize happily when contented or pleasurably stimulated.

COM 03M E **Vocalizes when talked to**
Credit is given if the client vocalizes happily when talked to by familiar persons. Persons at this level respond to the social conversation of familiar persons by laughing, squealing, or making other inarticulate vocalizations.

06 MONTHS
COM 06M A **Makes noise with objects**
Credit is given if the client uses objects to make noise. Persons at this level typically enjoy making

noise with objects and do so with or without encouragement. Examples of noise making behaviors include responses such as banging a toy on a hard surface or ringing a bell.

COM 06M B Turns head toward sound

Credit is given if the client turns head toward the source of a sound, especially the sound of a voice. Persons at this level are able to attend to sounds for periods of at least 10 seconds.

COM 06M C Vocalizes several different sounds

Credit is given if the client vocalizes several different vowels and consonants. Persons at this level are able to vocalize several different syllables consisting of vowels interspersed with consonants. However, vowels are still the dominant sounds made. Typical consonant vocalizations include ma, da, sh, ga, fa, and ba.

COM 06M D Communicates wants

Credit is given if the client is able to communicate specific wants through gestures and vocalizations. Persons at this level are able to express conscious wants by fussing, crying, and reaching out. Typical communications include crying when a familiar person leaves, crying when confronted by a stranger, reaching out toward a person they want attention from, reaching out for an object they want, and fussing when a desired object is taken from them.

COM 06M E Repeats own sound when sound is imitated

Credit is given if the client repeats own sound after that sound is imitated by another person. Persons at this level usually aren't imitating the words or sounds of others, but do imitate their own sounds when repeated by others.

12 MONTHS

COM 12M A Identifies one common object

Credit is given if the client names or identifies one common object. Persons at this level are able to identify at least one object either by saying its name or by pointing to it in repsonse to hearing it named.

COM 12M B Attends when directed

Credit is given if the client attends to objects or persons when directed. Persons at this level respond to directions such as "look at me", "look at the picture", and "listen to me".

COM 12M C **Says two words**

Credit is given if the client says or signs two words other than dada or mama. Persons at this level generally have an expressive vocabulary of at least two words not counting dada or mama. Typical words spoken include no, baby, bye-bye, hi, see, and bow-wow.

COM 12M D **Indicates wants**

Credit is given if the client indicates wants by using specific gestures or sounds. Persons at this level are able to express wants by means such as pointing with finger or hand at desired object, saying no, and shaking head for no.

COM 12M E **Imitates words or gestures**

Credit is given if the client imitates words, signs, or gestures. Persons at this level are able to imitate a few simple expressions which they see or hear. Examples include saying or signing words such as mama, dada, or baby in imitation, and waving bye-bye in imitation.

18 MONTHS

COM 18M A **Points to pictures of objects**

Credit is given if the client points to pictures of several common objects. Persons at this level, when presented with pictures of several objects, are able to point to the correct picture when the object is named. Typical objects identified at this level include pictures such as spoon, ball, cup, baby, and doggie.

COM 18M B **Uses gestures to help reinforce language**

Credit is given if the client uses gestures combined with spoken language. Persons at this level commonly use gestures while talking to help reinforce expressive communication. Examples of combining gestures and language include shaking head and saying no; pointing while verbally calling attention to events or objects; and pulling on arm while asking someone to follow.

COM 18M C Says ten words

Credit is given if the client says or signs about 10 words. Some typical words valued as survival concepts include potty, eat, no, yes, hurt, hot, drink, water, go, come, and bed.

COM 18M D Uses words for wants

Credit is given if the client uses words or signs to indicate wants. Persons at this level typically make wants known by naming the object desired or using simple action words. Common object and action words used include milk, cookie, more, gimme, up, down, now and mine.

COM 18M E Responds to simple directions

Credit is given if the client responds to simple directions. Persons at this level are able to respond to one-step directions such as sit down, wipe your nose, give me your hand, open your mouth, come here, and go to the bathroom.

02 YEARS

COM 02Y A Scores at 2-year level on picture vocabulary test

Credit is given if the client either (1) obtains a score of at least 2.0 years on a standardized picture recognition test such as the Peabody Picture Vocabulary Test (PPVT), or (2) identifies pictures described as typical of this level. Persons at this level are able to point to pictures of familiar objects when named. Typical familiar objects recognized include cup, shoe, ball, car, boat, horse, dog, cat, cow, chair, bed, etc.

COM 02Y B Listens to stories

Credit is given if the client listens attentively to short stories, songs, or nursery rhymes. Persons at this level are interested in watching children's shows on TV, listening to records of repetitive songs or nursery rhymes, and hearing stories about themselves and their familiar belongings. Typically, attention span is short, and only parts of songs or stories may hold the person's interest.

COM 02Y C Names familiar things

Credit is given if the client names or signs familiar objects. Persons at this level can name almost

everything he or she has daily contact with at home
or on excursions. An expressive vocabulary of 50
words or more is not uncommon.

COM 02Y D **Says two-word sentences**
Credit is given if the client verbalizes or signs immediate experiences or wants in sentences or
phrases of two to three words. Typical sentences include combinations such as "I want more, cup all
gone, go bus ride, and see baby."

COM 02Y E **Uses pronouns**
Credit is given if the client makes use of pronouns.
Persons at this level make use of pronouns such as I,
me, and you. Pronouns are used in combination with
other words in simple phrases but are not necessarily
used correctly.

03 YEARS

COM 03Y A **Scores at 3-year level on picture vocabulary test**
Credit is given if the client either (1) obtains a score
of at least 3.0 years on a standardized picture
recognition test such as the PPVT, or (2) identifies
pictures described as typical of this level. Persons at
this level are able to point to pictures of familiar objects and concepts when named. Typical familiar pictures recognized include eating, sitting, climbing, hit-
ting, fly, ant, snake, ladder, fish, bird, hammer, leaf,
catching, table, walking, sitting, etc.

COM 03Y B **Answers simple questions**
Credit is given if the client answers a few simple
questions. Persons at this level are able to give rele-
vant answers consisting of single words and short
phrases. Questions commonly answered include,
"What is the girl doing?", "Where are you going?",
"What is your name?", "How old are you?", and
"What is this?".

COM 03Y C **Gives simple account of experience**
Credit is given if the client gives simple account of
experiences either spontaneously or in response to
questioning. Descriptions of experiences at this level
usually consist of a single statement and often only
the last experience of a chain of events is described.
Examples of experiences described include, "I played

on the swing", "We went fishing", "We saw puppies", "I got sick", and "We went for a ride".

COM 03Y D Recites part of song or rhyme
Credit is given if the client has memorized and can recite all or parts of a few simple nursery rhymes, prayers, pledges, or songs. Persons at this level are able to recall and recite "catchy" verses spontaneously as well as in response to suggestion.

COM 03Y E Performs academic skills at nursery school level
Credit is given if the client either (1) scores at the nursery school level on a standardized academic achievement test such as the Wide Range Achievement Test (WRAT), or (2) performs academic skills described as typical of this level. Persons at this level perform typical nursery school skills such as counting two objects, counting by rote to five, identifying a few capital letters, giving the correct number of items requested up to two items, and repeating three digits by immediate recall.

04 YEARS

COM 04Y A Scores at 4-year level on picture vocabulary test
Credit is given if the client either (1) obtains a score of at least 4.0 years on a standardized picture recognition test such as the PPVT, or (2) identifies pictures described as typical of this level. Persons at this level are able to point to named pictures representing familiar objects and concepts. Typical pictures correctly identified include the common colors (red, white, blue, green, black, and yellow), emotions of happy and sad (pictures of faces), most zoo animals, and most common household objects.

COM 04Y B Tells use of common objects
Credit is given if the client answers questions concerning the use of common objects. Persons at this level are able to answer questions such as "What are clothes for?" (to keep us warm) and "What is money for?" (to buy candy).

COM 04Y C Says five-word long sentences
Credit is given if the client says sentences of five to six words in length. Persons at this level are able to say complete sentences such as "Can I come to your party?" or "My dog had two puppies."

COM 04Y D **Repeats nine-word long sentences**
Credit is given if the client repeats by immediate recall, sentences of 9 to 10 words in length (about 12 syllables).

COM 04Y E **Performs academic skills at pre-kindergarten level**
Credit is given if the client either (1) performs at the pre-kindergarten level on a standardized academic achievement test such as the WRAT, or (2) performs academic skills described as typical of this level. Typical skills performed at this level include copying a few capital letters, counting three objects, and counting by rote to 10.

05 YEARS

COM 05Y A **Scores at 5-year level on picture vocabulary test**
Credit is given if the client either (1) obtains a score of at least 5.0 years on a standardized picture recognition test such as the PPVT, or (2) identifies pictures described as typical of this level. Persons at this level are able to pick out pictures representing familiar objects and concepts when named. Typical pictures recognized include parts of objects such as hands of a clock, specific coins (penny, nickel, dime, quarter), many wild animals not found in the zoo, and everyday-type activities such as shopping and gardening.

COM 05Y B **Asks questions to seek information**
Credit is given if the client asks meaningful questions to seek information rather than just to make conversation.

COM 05Y C **Gives detailed account of experience**
Credit is given if the client is able to recall and describe a recent experience in some detail. Persons at this level are able to relate recent experiences with relevant detail, including proper sequence, when it happened, where it happened and who was involved.

COM 05Y D **Defines simple words**
Credit is given if the client is able to define simple words. Persons at this level typically define familiar objects in terms of use. For example, a chair is something you sit on; a pencil is something you write with; air is something you breathe; and a spoon is what you eat with.

COM 05Y E Performs academic skills at the kindergarten level
Credit is given if the client either (1) scores at the kindergarten level on a standardized academic achievement test such as the WRAT, or (2) performs academic skills described as typical of this level. Typical skills performed at this level include recognizing and printing first name, identifying several numbers, counting 10 objects, copying numbers, writing a few numbers from dictation, naming several coins, and identifying words on familiar signs.

08 YEARS

COM 08Y A Scores at 8-year level on picture vocabulary test
Credit is given if the client either (1) obtains a score of at least 8.0 years on a standardized picture recognition test such as the PPVT, or (2) identifies pictures described as typical of this level. Persons at this level are able to pick out pictures representing familiar objects and concepts when named. Typical pictures recognized include various emotions (love, delight, hate, grief, etc.), rituals and life happenings (marriage, funeral, birth, death, worship, illness, etc.), foreign lands, and recreational and sporting activities.

COM 08Y B States how objects are alike and not alike
Credit is given if the client can describe the similarities and differences between familiar objects. Persons at this level are able to answer questions such as "How are a stick and a tree alike and how are they different?" Typical responses include answers such as they are both made of wood; a tree is alive while a stick isn't; or a tree grows and a stick doesn't.

COM 08Y C Reads and uses simple instructions
Credit is given if the client can read and use simple "how to" instructions. Persons at this level are able to read and use instructions written at the third grade level of difficulty. Typical instructions read and used, include those found on simple toys requiring assembly from a few parts.

COM 08Y D Uses telephone routinely
Credit is given if the client uses the telephone routinely for social use. Persons at this level are able

to dial numbers quickly and accurately. Usually the numbers dialed are memorized or written down for easy reference.

COM 08Y E **Performs academic skills at the 3rd grade level**
Credit is given if the client either (1) scores at the third grade level on a standardized academic achievement test such as the WRAT, or (2) performs academic skills described as typical of this level. Persons at this level are able to read and write simple sentences; perform some addition, subtraction, and multiplication; measure distance in feet; and tell how many pennies are in various coins.

12 YEARS

COM 12Y A **Reads for information and enjoyment**
Credit is given if the client is able to read a variety of written material for both information and entertainment. Persons at this level are able to read and use magazines, books, newspapers, and other materials written at the seventh grade level of difficulty.

COM 12Y B **Writes short, meaningful letters**
Credit is given if the client writes short letters which convey significant information. Persons at this level generally write letters thanking others for gifts or describing what has been happening recently in their lives. Typical letters are written to pen pals, friends and relatives. The letters are meaningful and envelopes are addressed with enough accuracy for the letters to arrive at the intended destination.

COM 12Y C **Describes a story in length with detail**
Credit is given if the client verbally describes a story, movie, or experience. Persons at this level are able to describe in length and with accurate detail.

COM 12Y D **Finds alphabetically indexed information**
Credit is given if the client is able to locate specific information in references and directories. Persons at this level are able to demonstrate the proper use of catalogues, dictionaries, encyclopedias, and telephone directories, including the yellow pages.

COM 12Y E **Performs academic skills at the 7th grade level**
Credit is given if the client either (1) scores at the seventh grade level on a standardized academic

achievement test such as the WRAT, or (2) performs academic skills described as typical of this level. Persons at this level are able to add and subtract fractions, convert decimals to percentage, and read and spell most words commonly used in conversation.

16 YEARS

COM 16Y A Discusses abstract and philosophical ideas
Credit is given if the client discusses current events and abstract philosophical issues and ideas. Persons at this level are able to follow, analyze, discuss, and speculate on topics such as political issues and world problems.

COM 16Y B Writes business letters
Credit is given if the client demonstrates knowledge and ability to prepare and send a business letter. Persons at this level are able to organize and write a formal business letter as part of a class assignment or when the need arises.

COM 16Y C Reads and uses complex instructions
Credit is given if the client can read and use complex "how to" instructions. Persons at this level are able to read and use instructions written at the tenth grade level of difficulty. Typical instructions read and used include those accompanying projects such as making garments, assembling a bicycle, making models from kits, tuning up an automobile engine, and following carpentry plans.

COM 16Y D Delivers formal speech
Credit is given if the client demonstrates the ability to research a topic and prepare and deliver a formal speech.

COM 16Y E Performs academic skills at the 10th grade level
Credit is given if the client either (1) scores at the tenth grade level on a standardized academic achievement test such as the WRAT, or (2) performs academic skills described as typical of this level. Persons at this level are able to multiply fractions, find averages, do long division, convert fractions to percentages, and read and comprehend most non-technical publications or literature prepared for use by the general public.

MOBILITY & DEXTERITY

03 MONTHS

M&D 03M A **Follows object or sound**
Credit is given if the client tracks moving objects or sounds with eyes or head. Persons at this level briefly attend to sights and sounds that move across the perceptual field.

M&D 03M B **Reaches for dangling object**
Credit is given if the client reaches for an interesting or attractive object which is dangled in front of the face. Persons at this level are able to reach for an object by making repeated movements in the direction of the sight or sound of the object.

M&D 03M C **Holds object placed in hand**
Credit is given if the client closes hand when touched by an object. Persons at this level are able to retain objects with a palmar grasp for short periods, up to 3 (three) minutes.

M&D 03M D **Supports upper body with arms**
Credit is given if the client elevates head and chest with arms when lying on abdomen. Persons at this level are able to hold chest up and head erect for 10 (ten) seconds.

M&D 03 E **Holds head steady**
Credit is given if the client holds head steady when in an upright position. Persons at this level are able to hold head erect with minimum head bobbing.

06 MONTHS

M&D 06M A **Stands with support**
Credit is given if the client stands with substantial support. Persons at this level are able to support own weight on feet but need to be held in order to maintain balance.

M&D 06M B **Handles objects**
Credit is given if the client actively manipulates objects with hands. Persons at this level are able to reach for and grasp objects within reach and may be

able to transfer objects from one hand to the other. Generally, these persons rotate wrists freely while manipulating objects.

M&D 06M C Moves backward or forward on abdomen

Credit is given if the client propels self on abdomen for a short distance. Persons at this level are able to move either backward or forward by twisting, rolling, wriggling, pushing with feet or arms, or pulling with hands.

M&D 06M D Rolls from back to stomach

Credit is given if the client rolls from back to stomach. Persons at this level are able to roll back and forth, from back to stomach and from stomach to back.

M&D 06M E Sits with little support

Credit is given if the client sits with little or no support for 30 seconds or more. Persons at this level may lean forward and use their hands to help maintain balance.

12 MONTHS

M&D 12M A Stands alone without assistance

Credit is given if the client stands alone well. Persons at this level are able to stoop and pick up objects off of the floor from a standing position without losing balance.

M&D 12M B Transfers small objects using pincer grasp

Credit is given if the client picks up a small object using a pincer grasp and transfers and releases voluntarily into a container. Persons at this level typically find this activity pleasurable and engage in this behavior unprompted with obvious intent.

M&D 12M C Performs fine motor tasks of 12-month level complexity

Credit is given if the client is able to perform simple fine motor tasks. Persons at this level perform skills such as marking with a crayon, turning pages of a book, or stacking two blocks.

M&D 12M D Stands or sits independently

Credit is given if the client stands up or sits down without assistance. Persons at this level are able to stand up from a lying position on back or stomach, or sit from a standing position without falling.

M&D 12M E **Ambulates by walking or creeping**
Credit is given if the client walks alone or with hand held or creeps with good coordination. Creeping generally starts earlier (approximately 7 months), but still may serve as the primary form of ambulation at this level.

18 MONTHS

M&D 18M A **Runs poorly or walks well**
Credit is given if the client runs (balance and coordination may be poor), or walks with good balance (coordination may be poor). Persons at this level may run with legs stiff or walk with a broad base, but assistance is not required.

M&D 18M B **Propels ball in forward direction**
Credit is given if the client is able to propel a ball in direction intended. Persons at this level are able to throw or kick a ball forward. The ball may be barely tossed or bounced, and the kick made by walking into the ball, but the intent of the effort is clearly to propel the object.

M&D 18M C **Performs fine motor tasks of 18-month level complexity.**
Credit is given if the client is able to perform 18-month level fine motor tasks. Persons at this level are able to perform skills such as stacking several blocks (3-4), making definite crayon strokes, or tearing paper.

M&D 18M D **Seats self on chair**
Credit is given if the client seats self on a chair. Persons at this level may sit by backing into the chair, but no assistance is required for size-appropriate chairs.

M&D 18M E **Walks up stairs assisted**
Credit is given if the client is able to walk up stairs by holding onto the railing or with hand held. Persons at this level are able to climb stairs in an upright position but may require support to prevent falling and typically take two steps per tread.

02 YEARS

M&D 02Y A Runs or jumps without falling

Credit is given if the client runs or jumps with good coordination. Persons at this level are able to run or jump (with both feet off the floor) without falling.

M&D 02Y B Balances on board or when crouching

Credit is given if the client demonstrates good balance by standing on the wide surface of a standard 2"x4" board or when in a crouch position. Persons at this level are able to get up without falling or balance with both feet on a 3½ to 4" wide board for 5 seconds.

M&D 02Y C Performs fine motor tasks of 2-year level complexity

Credit is given if the client is able to perform 2-year level fine motor tasks. Persons at this level are able to perform skills such as stacking 6 to 7 blocks, imitating vertical and horizontal crayon strokes, making a single fold in a piece of paper, or turning single pages in a book.

M&D 02Y D Opens door

Credit is given if the client is able to open familiar doors. Persons at this level open doors by turning the door knob (with one or both hands, depending on the size of the knob), and then pushing or pulling on the door.

M&D 02Y E Walks up stairs unaided or down stairs aided

Credit is given if the client walks up stairs alone without using the rail or down stairs with or without help. Persons at this level generally take two steps per tread.

03 YEARS

M&D 03Y A Stands or hops on one foot

Credit is given if the client stands or hops on one foot for a short period. Persons at this level are able to stand on one foot momentarily (at least 2-3 seconds) or hop on one foot for a short distance (2-3 hops).

M&D 03Y B Rides a pedal toy

Credit is given if the client rides a tricycle or other pedal device. Persons at this level are able to pedal proficiently and can ride pedal toys and devices not requiring special balancing.

M&D 03Y C   **Performs fine motor tasks of 3-year level complexity**

Credit is given if the client is able to perform 3-year level fine motor tasks. Persons at this level are able to perform skills such as copying a circle and a cross, or cutting paper with scissors. The cross and circle need not be exact reproductions, but should be recognizable. Any intentional cut made with scissors is credited.

M&D 03Y D   **Throws object with some accuracy**

Credit is given if the client throws a ball with enough accuracy to be caught by an adult standing five to seven feet away or throws a bean bag into a 12-inch hole at a distance of three to four feet.

M&D 03Y E   **Alternates feet going up stairs**

Credit is given if the client alternates feet when walking up stairs. Persons at this level are able to climb stairs in an adult fashion without assistance or support.

04 YEARS

M&D 04Y A   **Gallops or performs standing or running jump**

Credit is given if the client demonstrates ability to skip with one foot (gallop) or performs a running broad jump of 23 to 33 inches or a standing broad jump of 8 to 10 inches.

M&D 04Y B   **Walks a line without stepping off**

Credit is given if the client can walk a path that is one inch wide without stepping off. Persons at this level are able to follow a straight 10-foot long path or a circular path which is 4 feet in diameter, without stepping off the line.

M&D 04Y C   **Performs fine motor tasks of 4-year level complexity**

Credit is given if the client is able to perform 4-year level fine motor tasks. Persons at this level are able to perform skills such as cutting with scissors on a line or drawing crude but recognizable designs, letters, or pictures with crayon or pencil. The drawings may be made with or without copying.

M&D 04Y D Carries cup of water or catches ball
Credit is given if the client carries a cup of water without spilling it or catches a bounced or tossed ball.

M&D 04Y E Alternates feet going down stairs
Credit is given if the client alternates feet going down stairs. Persons at this level are able to climb and descend stairs in an adult fashion without need for support or assistance.

05 YEARS

M&D 05Y A Skips correctly or hops on one foot
Credit is given if the client skips using feet alternately or hops on one foot with good balance. Persons at this level are able to skip with good coordination or hop on one foot for a distance of 16 feet.

M&D 05Y B Walks on board
Credit is given if the client balances and walks on the wide part of a standard 2"x4" board. Persons at this level are able to walk a distance of 6 feet on a 3½ to 4" wide walking board in 10-seconds without falling off.

M&D 05Y C Performs fine motor tasks of 5-year level complexity
Credit is given if the client is able to perform 5-year level fine motor tasks. Persons at this level are able to perform skills such as copying simple geometric designs (i.e., asterick type star, rectangle, triangle) or colors within a marked area such as the outline of a picture or imitates making a diagonal fold in a piece of paper.

M&D 05Y D Balances on toes or one foot
Credit is given if the client is able to balance on toes for 3 to 5 seconds or walks 10 feet on toes without touching heels to the floor, or stands on one foot for 8 seconds or more.

M&D 05Y E Runs 35 yards or kicks ball through the air
Credit is given if the client performs a 35-yard dash or kicks a ball off of the ground. Persons at this level are able to run 35 yards in 10 seconds or less, or kick a soccer ball 8 to 11½ feet through the air.

08 YEARS

M&D 08Y A   Hits ball with bat, racquet or paddle
Credit is given if the client hits a pitched softball with a bat or serves and returns a tennis or ping pong ball. Inexperienced persons may require several tries to hit the ball to the proper spot.

M&D 08Y B   Balances on bicycle or skates
Credit is given if the client rides a bicycle or uses roller skates or ice skates. Persons at this level have good balance and are able to operate a bicycle or use skates if given the opportunity.

M&D 08Y C   Writes or prints legible words and sentences
Credit is given if the client writes or prints words and sentences which can be easily read. Persons at this level are able to accurately write letters, numbers, words and sentences. They are able to write sentences, maintaining fairly uniform letter size, spacing, slant, alignment, and separation between words.

M&D 08Y D   Demonstrates the crawl swimming stroke
Credit is given if the client swims using the crawl stroke or demonstrates an approximation of the crawl stroke by kicking feet simultaneously with the overhand arm movement. Credit may also be given if the client demonstrates raising the opposite leg and arm alternately, while in a standing position.

M&D 08Y E   Bounces and catches ball with one hand
Credit is given if the client bounces and catches a ball using only one hand. Persons at this level are able to bounce the ball from the floor and catch the ball as it descends into the hand with palm up. This skill usually is executed successfully with the dominant hand.

12 YEARS

M&D 12Y A   Plays musical instrument
Credit is given if the client is able to play a recognizable song on a musical instrument. Persons at this level are able to pick out a simple melody on an instrument such as a piano or xylophone, even if they have not had formal lessons on an instrument.

M&D 12Y B Throws softball

Credit is given if the client throws a softball with enough accuracy and distance to participate and contribute to a softball game. Boys can throw a ball from one base to another in a single flight; girls may require one or two bounces. The average maximum distance for the softball throw is 110 feet for boys and 60 feet for girls.

M&D 12Y C Pulls up or hangs on a bar

Credit is given if the client is able to do at least one correct pull-up or hang for 10 seconds from an over-the-head bar. Boys at this level are able to do two or more pull-ups using an overhand grip; girls are able to hang from the bar with arms extended for at least 10 seconds.

M&D 12Y D Performs standing broad jump

Credit is given if the client is able to perform a standing broad jump, using correct stance and motion. Persons at this level typically perform a jump of at least 5 feet for boys or 4½ feet for girls.

M&D 12Y E Performs 50-yard dash

Credit is given if the client runs a distance of 50 yards in 10 seconds or less. Persons at this level typically perform a 50-yard dash within 8 seconds for boys and 9 seconds for girls.

16 YEARS

M&D 16Y A Participates in competitive sport

Credit is given if the client applies physical skills in a competitive sport or contest. Persons at this level commonly participate in competitive activities such as tennis, baseball, basketball, gymnastics or soccer.

M&D 16Y B Ties several different knots

Credit is given if the client is able to make practical use of several different knots. Persons at this level typically tie the granny knot, square knot, and slip knot. Knowledge of additional knots is common, depending on individual experiences.

M&D 16Y C Operates device requiring complex skills

Credit is given if the client operates devices requiring complex dexterity skills. Persons at this level typically have mastered at least one device such as a musical instrument, typewriter, video game, or one of various other types of tools or machinery.

M&D 16Y D **Dances with another person**

Credit is given if the client is able to perform at least one recognizable dance step with another person. Persons at this level have had some exposure to dancing and are able to lead/follow to music, using common dance steps such as fox trot, waltz, pop, or western.

M&D 16Y E **Qualifies for driving automobile**

Credit is given if the client completes a course in driver training or obtains a driving license by passing a driver licensing examination.

VOCATION & RECREATION

03 MONTHS

V&R 03M A **Inspects surroundings within room**
Credit is given if the client inspects surroundings both close up and across the room. Persons at this level inspect things such as lights, windows, and people for periods up to ten seconds.

V&R 03M B **Shows interest in dangling object**
Credit is given if the client exhibits obvious signs of interest in a dangling object. Persons at this level are attracted by unusual objects, especially if the objects are colorful, moving, and very close (within 18 inches). Typically, interest is evidenced by the client looking at or reaching for the object.

V&R 03M C **Anticipates return of toy**
Credit is given if the client quiets while waiting for the return of a toy or other interesting object. Persons at this level stop body movement and briefly track the person returning a toy or object which has been dropped or taken away. Movement of arms, legs, and head resume upon receipt of the object.

V&R 03M D **Engages in non-directed physical activities**
Credit is given if the client engages in nondirected physical activities when not attended. Persons at this level spend their unstructured awake time engaged in activities such as kicking, rotating head from side to side, rolling from side to side, and waving arms.

V&R 03M E **Plays with fingers**
Credit is given if the client plays with or displays interest in own fingers. Persons at this level typically exhibit interest by engaging in activities such as clasping and unclasping hands, mutual fingering play, looking at hand, and filtering or catching light with fingers.

06 MONTHS

V&R 06M A Inspects and manipulates
Credit is given if the client inspects and manipulates objects. Persons at this level are able to see, reach for, and pick up objects. Objects are visually inspected, felt, tasted, banged, dropped, transferred from hand-to-hand, etc.

V&R 06M B Reaches promptly for seen objects
Credit is given if the client reaches promptly and persistently for seen objects. Persons at this level are able to pick up objects directly in a smooth coordinated motion.

V&R 06M C Entertains self unattended for 15 minutes
Credit is given if the client entertains self unattended for 15 minutes or more. Persons at this level spend some of their unstructured time engaged in activities such as playing with toys, moving hand across field of vision, creeping, sitting, and rolling. Prolonged toy play may require a series of toys, as interest in a single toy is typically of short duration.

V&R 06M D Engages in gross motor exercises
Credit is given if the client engages in directed gross motor exercises. Persons at this level engage in purposeful motor activities such as crawling, kicking, extending legs upward, grasping feet, or pulling off stockings.

V&R 06M E Engages in play with toys
Credit is given if the client engages spontaneously in play with toys. Persons at this level are attracted by small objects such as string, paper, soft squeaky toys, rattles, spoons, cups, and blocks.

12 MONTHS

V&R 12M A Watches scenery on excursions
Credit is given if the client follows the movements of pedestrians and inspects the landscape during excursions such as motor vehicle rides and walks.

V&R 12M B Imitates simple demonstrations
Credit is given if the client gives crude reproductions of simple demonstrations. Persons at this level are able to repeat very simple actions performed by others. The complexity of acts imitated is illustrated

by tasks such as stacking 2 or 3 blocks, hammering pegs with a wooden hammer, holding a watch to ear, putting objects into a container, and pushing a toy car.

V&R 12M C **Plays unattended for 30 minutes with toys**
Credit is given if the client occupies self unattended for 30 to 60 minutes with manipulative toys. The complexity of typical play at this level is illustrated by activities such as putting clothespins in and out of a basket, looking at and fingering buttons, taking covers off of containers, and stacking objects.

V&R 12M D **Plays unattended for 30 minutes in gross motor exercises**
Credit is given if the client occupies self unattended for 30 to 60 minutes with gross motor activities. Typical gross motor activities at this level include exercises such as pulling self to standing position, creeping, crawling up and down stairs, lowering self to sitting position, and walking around while holding onto objects.

V&R 12M E **Plays with several small objects at one time**
Credit is given if the client engages in play utilizing several small objects at one time. Persons at this level are able to retain two objects while picking up a third, pick up several objects and then drop them one-by-one, and hold an object with one hand while exploring with the other.

18 MONTHS

V&R 18M A **Points to objects of interest**
Credit is given if the client points at interesting sights during excursions such as walks and rides. Typical interesting sights at this level include objects such as airplanes, animals, the moon, bicycle riders, and trains.

V&R 18M B **Imitates domestic tasks**
Credit is given if the client mimics domestic tasks. Persons at this level attempt to sweep, dust, wipe up puddles, etc. Typical efforts are highly unsuccessful but are obvious attempts at imitation.

V&R 18M C **Plays alone for up to 60 minutes**
Credit is given if the client amuses self for 30 to 60 minutes with toys of own choosing. Persons at this level are especially entertained by play activities involving a sandbox or wading pool and enthusiastically fill and empty containers with sand or water.

V&R 18M D **Performs simple tasks in home**
Credit is given if the client performs simple tasks in the home when directed by both words and gestures. Persons at this level are able to fetch objects that are nearby and in plain view, return items to place of storage, hand an item to a nearby person, discard a piece of paper in a waste basket, etc.

V&R 18M E **Manipulates objects in intended manner**
Credit is given if the client uses objects in intended manner. Persons at this level are able to cause in-tended effect with objects requiring one-action manipulations. Typical one-action manipulations include pulling or pushing a wheel toy, turning the knob on a radio or musical toy, flipping a light switch, or closing a door.

02 YEARS

V&R 02Y A **Performs simple tasks in home**
Credit is given if the client performs simple tasks in the home when directed by words or gestures. Persons at this level perform tasks such as fetching familiar objects from another room when asked, attempting to fold laundry items, and using a chair to obtain out-of-reach objects.

V&R 02Y B **Imitates adult tasks with toys**
Credit is given if the client mimics adult tasks with toys or other objects such as tools, garden equipment, household appliances, or dolls. Persons at this level imitate adult tasks as a form of play.

V&R 02Y C **Operates action toys**
Credit is given if the client operates toys which respond to proper manipulations by moving or producing a sound. Persons at this level are able to operate action toys such as a telephone, windup toys, soap bubble maker, or egg beater. Fragile toys, typically, are broken right away.

V&R 02Y D **Engages in gross motor play**
Credit is given if the client engages in gross motor activities such as climbing on boxes, turning in circles to music, riding a kiddy car and pushing with feet, pushing large objects, or rocking in a rocking chair or on a hobby horse. Persons at this level are highly geared to gross motor activities and recognize the play potential of climbing objects, vehicles, and rocking toys after an initial introduction.

V&R 02Y E **Engages in sedentary play**
Credit is given if the client engages in sedentary play involving activities such as stacking blocks, looking at pictures in picture books, marking with crayon or pencil, listening to adult conversations, or watching peers at play.

03 YEARS

V&R 03Y A **Helps in home**
Credit is given if the client assists with domestic tasks such as making two folds in a towel, picking up toys, straightening bedcover, sweeping off walk, drying dishes, or dusting. Persons at this level help when asked, but their assistance is of poor quality.

V&R 03Y B **Engages in pretend play**
Credit is given if the client engages in solitary imaginative play on own initiative or when prompted. Persons at this level are able to engage in pretend play utilizing concrete objects to help structure the imagined situation. Imagined situations include pretending to be an engineer of a toy train, pretending to be a cowboy while riding a hobby horse, pretending to be a mother while playing with a doll, etc.

V&R 03Y C **Engages in creative play**
Credit is given if the client engages in creative play with materials such as sand, mud, or clay. Persons at this level create on own initiative or after demonstration. Typical creations include pies, cakes, roads, tunnels, balls, etc.

V&R 03Y D **Uses gross motor equipment**
Credit is given if the client utilizes gross motor equipment such as swings, jungle gym, teeter totter, tricy-

cle, wagon, or slide. Persons at this level employ gross motor equipment in manner intended but may require assistance or supervision, especially with items such as swings, slides, and teeter totters.

V&R 03Y E Engages in sedentary activities

Credit is given if the client plays sedentarily for extended periods of time. Persons at this level are able to entertain themselves for up to 90 minutes with activities such as listening to stories or records, building structures with blocks, assembling simple formboard puzzles, painting or coloring using assorted colors, or watching favorite programs on TV.

04 YEARS

V&R 04Y A Runs short errands

Credit is given if the client runs a variety of errands within home and immediate neighborhood. Persons at this level run errands such as delivering items to nearby neighbors, fetching items from nearby residences, or bringing desired objects to parents/siblings.

V&R 04Y B Engages in dramatic play

Credit is given if the client combines dramatic play with simple materials. Persons at this level are able to engage in pretend play with objects that are unlike the objects imagined. Examples of dramatized situations include imagining blocks to be items of food during store play, pretending that a chair is a house, pretending that a broom is a horse, constructing animate or inanimate objects with blocks, etc.

V&R 04Y C Plays alone for two hours

Credit is given if the client plays contentedly by self for up to two hours at a time. Persons at this level entertain themselves for prolonged periods with purposeful play involving gross motor or fine motor activities. (For examples of constructive play, see items V&R 04Y D and V&R 04Y E)

V&R 04Y D Uses gross motor equipment

Credit is given if the client uses gross motor equipment (see V&R 03Y D). Persons at this level employ gross motor equipment in the manner intended and require little assistance or supervision.

V&R 04Y E Engages in sedentary manual tasks
Credit is given if the client engages in tasks requiring fine motor control. Persons at this level engage in such activities as drawing and painting crude pictures/letters/designs; cutting out a design with scissors; making detailed constructions with blocks; or hammering nails into a board.

05 YEARS

V&R 05Y A Helps about the home
Credit is given if the client helps about the home with simple chores such as picking up and vacuuming a room, feeding and dressing a younger or less capable person, drying dishes, seting the table, hosing off a sidewalk, using a squeegee mop, or polishing furniture. Persons at this level are able to do useful work but perform best when working along with an adult.

V&R 05Y B Carries out preplanned projects
Credit is given if the client carries out projects that were previously conceived or were proposed by parents, siblings, friends, etc. Persons at this level are able to build a recognizable object out of blocks, make a drawing of an animal, nail scraps of wood together to resemble a boat or box, etc.

V&R 05Y C Completes activity
Credit is given if the client completes one activity before going on to the next. Persons at this level generally complete a task before switching to another. They are interested in seeing finished products and, unless a task is too difficult or lengthy, attempt to see it to completion. Jumping from task-to-task or activity-to-activity is characteristic of an earlier level of maturity.

V&R 05Y D Engages in gross motor activities
Credit is given if the client engages is gross motor activities such as climbing trees, roller skating, jumping rope, swinging well (pumps using legs), and marching or keeping time to music. Persons at this level are able to perform more complex and varied activities than at previous levels.

V&R 05Y E **Performs fine motor tasks**
Credit is given if the client engages in tasks requiring fine motor skills. Persons at this level are able to perform tasks such as sewing along a line, nailing boards together, putting on a record, building structures from tinker toys or toy building logs, sawing a board in half, or unlocking a padlock with a key.

08 YEARS
V&R 08Y A **Performs useful chores**
Credit is given if the client performs useful chores on a routine basis with minimal supervision. Persons at this level are able to wash dishes, set the table, make beds, dust, vacuum, feed animals, etc. Monetary compensation is generally not received at this level unless as an allowance.

V&R 08Y B **Uses simple tools**
Credit is given if the client makes practical use of simple tools. Examples include chopping weeds with a hoe, digging a hole for planting, hammering loose nails, screwing in a loose doorknob, shoveling snow, raking leaves, hemming a straight edge, or crocheting with a chain stitch.

V&R 08Y C **Reads simple material for recreation**
Credit is given if the client reads simple written material for recreational purposes. Persons at this level read materials such as game instructions, comics, movie titles, simple stories, or simple how-to instructions.

V&R 08Y D **Engages in a variety of play activities**
Credit is given if the client engages in a variety of play activities which require repetitive practice for mastery. Examples of typical activities mastered at this level include rowing a boat, skating, swimming, flying a kite, operating a yo-yo, playing marbles, shooting baskets, or bowling.

V&R 08Y E **Assembles toys**
Credit is given if the client assembles toys without assistance following simple directions. Persons at this level assemble toys such as snap-together model kits, erector sets, jigsaw puzzles, kites, cereal box toys, or paper/balsa airplanes.

12 YEARS

V&R 12Y A **Performs responsible tasks for pay**
Credit is given if the client performs responsible tasks, often for monetary compensation. Persons at this level are able to perform useful work and commonly do work for parents or neighbors in return for pay. Typical work includes tasks such as cleaning the garage, having a paper route, pulling nails, baby sitting, performing simple cooking or ironing, mowing the lawn, cleaning house, or pulling weeds.

V&R 12Y B **Budgets allowance or earnings**
Credit is given if the client budgets small sums of money from allowance or earnings to cover expenditures for entertainment, school supplies, bus fare, school lunches, special purchases, etc.

V&R 12Y C **Plans and carries out project**
Credit is given if the client plans, organizes, and successfully executes an activity or project without adult assistance. Persons at this level are able to plan and carryout an activity such as a picnic, meal, school project, money making scheme, or party.

V&R 12Y D **Performs activities requiring complex skills**
Credit is given if the client engages in a variety of activities requiring complex skills. Persons at this level are able to perform tasks requiring integration of manual and conceptual skills. Examples of activities mastered include building projects such as constructing a simple fort or tree house, playing a musical instrument, casting with a spinning reel and rod, practicing with a rifle, or building model cars or planes.

V&R 12Y E **Performs simple creative work**
Credit is given if the client performs simple creative work. Persons at this level are able to perform creative tasks such as knitting scarves, sewing simple clothing with a sewing machine, making useful items in a woodshop using hand tools, writing stories or poems, or creating graphic designs or paintings.

16 YEARS

V&R 16Y A **Performs responsible employment**
Credit is given if the client holds down a responsible paying job when not in school. Persons at this level

typically have worked at one or more part-time or temporary jobs. Examples of typical employment include summer camp counselor, baby sitter, usher, store clerk, gas station attendant, house painter, farm hand, carpenter's helper, box person, lifeguard, etc.

V&R 16Y B Understands essential economics

Credit is given if the client demonstrates awareness of essential economics for independent living. Persons at this level are able to describe, demonstrate, or make routine use of practices such as checking and savings accounts, budgeting income, insurance, loans, or time payments.

V&R 16Y C Displays appropriate job-readiness skills

Credit is given if the client displays appropriate job-readiness skills including knowledge of sources of job leads, filling out an application form, phoning for an appointment, presenting self acceptably for an interview, demonstrating consistent punctuality, accepting criticism, etc.

V&R 16Y D Describes variety of jobs and requirements

Credit is given if the client describes a variety of occupations and the prerequisite skills, education, or training necessary for their attainment. Persons at this level are able to describe the requirements for common occupations such as doctor, mechanic, lawyer, craftsman, engineer, teacher, nurse, businessman, or secretary.

V&R 16Y E Builds or repairs with adult skill

Credit is given if the client makes or maintains items requiring adult level skills. Persons at this level are able to perform tasks such as building a stereo cabinet, constructing a coat or dress, knitting a sweater, repairing or arranging for the repair of a car or appliance, or maintaining a house.

SOCIALIZATION

03 MONTHS

SOC 03M A **Indicates need for attention**
Credit is given if the client indicates a desire for human companionship. Persons at this level indicate this need for social attention by protesting when left alone or quieting or relaxing when approached or attended.

SOC 03M B **Makes eye contact**
Credit is given if the client makes eye contact, briefly, with a familiar person. Persons at this level look at and visually search and inspect familiar faces.

SOC 03M C **Watches people**
Credit is given if the client looks at or watches people and their activities for brief periods.

SOC 03M D **Smiles responsively**
Credit is given if the client smiles at familiar persons. Persons at this level, typically, smile and vocalize in response to the social approach of a familiar person or the sight of a familiar face.

SOC 03M E **Listens to voices**
Credit is given if the client attends to the sound of the human voice. Persons at this level quiet or turn head when people talk or sing and may search with eyes for the source of a voice.

06 MONTHS

SOC 06M A **Indicates desire for companionship**
Credit is given if the client indicates a need or desire for human companionship. Persons at this level indicate this need by actions such as extending arms toward people with apparent intent to be picked up or otherwise attended to, following the caretaker, or calling for help by vocalizing in some fashion.

SOC 06M B **Responds positively to familiar persons**
Credit is given if the client makes positive responses to familiar persons. Persons at this level smile, laugh, pat, touch or otherwise respond positively to the sight, approach, or touch of familiar persons.

SOC 06M C Participates in social play

Credit is given if the client participates in reciprocal social play. Persons at this level respond by hiding face during game of "peek-a-boo," respond physically and verbally to game of "I'm-going-to-get-you," spread or raise arms in response to the game "How-big-are-you," etc.

SOC 06M D Smiles in response to smile

Credit is given if the client smiles in response to being smiled at by another person.

SOC 06M E Distinguishes adults from children

Credit is given if the client differentiates between caretakers and younger or less capable persons. Persons at this level typically enjoy other childern such as older siblings but tend to be more demanding of parental or adult attention.

12 MONTHS

SOC 12M A Indicates desire for companionship

Credit is given if the client indicates a need or desire for human companionship. Persons at this level indicate this need by actions such as grasping or holding the hand of another, tugging on clothing, hugging others, or climbing on the lap of another.

SOC 12M B Shows affection when cued

Credit is given if the client shows affection to person, pet, or toy animal when requested. Persons at this level show affection by smiling, patting, touching, or hugging persons, animals, or toys in response to suggestion or in imitation.

SOC 12M C Participates in social games

Credit is given if the client participates in social games such as where-is-the-baby, being chased, waving bye-bye, or game of up-and-down-with-arms.

SOC 12M D Participates in give-and-take play routines

Credit is given if the client participates in give-and-take play with others. Examples of give-and-take play routines include repeatedly giving and taking back some object, back-and-forth rolling of a ball, throwing things to have them returned, fetching items that have been tossed, etc.

SOC 12M E **Enjoys social walks**
Credit is given if the client participates in social walks with obvious enjoyment. Persons at this level generally come readily when asked if they want to go for a walk.

18 MONTHS

SOC 18M A **Engages in supervised parallel play**
Credit is given if the client engages in supervised parallel play for short periods. Persons at this level are able to play in the company of peers without problems for at least 5 minutes. Play tends to be solitary, but company is valued as evidenced by upset or following when the companion leaves.

SOC 18M B **Seeks another for specific purpose**
Credit is given if the client seeks out another person for a specific purpose. Persons at this level initiate interactions because of needs and wants. Typical interactions include bringing a cup to get a drink, bringing a broken possession for assistance, bringing a shoe for help in dressing, etc.

SOC 18M C **Participates in group activity**
Credit is given if the client participates in family-like group activities for short periods. Persons at this level participate in group activities such as shopping trips, meals at a common table, picnics, trip to the zoo, etc. Participation is typically limited to going along with whatever the group is doing, but pleasure in the experience is apparent.

SOC 18M D **Helps family member when directed**
Credit is given if the client helps perform simple tasks when directed by family members or other familiar persons. For examples of typical domestic commissions, see item V&R 18M D.

SOC 18M E **Pretends social behavior with toys when cued**
Credit is given if the client engages in simplified play with puppets, stuffed animals, or dolls when directed. Persons at this level are able to interact with figures of persons or animals. Typical pretend play includes interactions such as laying a doll on a bed, covering a doll with a blanket, touching a doll's mouth with a spoon, or touching a doll's head with a comb.

02 YEARS

SOC 02Y A Plays in parallel for 20 minutes
Credit is given if the client engages in unsupervised parallel play for a period of 20 minutes or longer. Persons at this level are able to enjoy the nearness of peers while engaging in individual play activities. Examples of parallel play activities include watching TV, coloring, filling containers with water or sand, etc.

SOC 02Y B Expresses affection without cues
Credit is given if the client shows affection to family members, friends, pet, or toy animal on own initiative.

SOC 02Y C Initiates greetings and farewells
Credit is given if the client responds to and initiates greetings and farewells. Persons at this level say or gesture expressions such as "hello" and "bye-bye."

SOC 02Y D Helps family members when directed
Credit is given if the client follows simple directives for tasks such as bringing named items to family members upon request. For other examples of domestic commissions, see V&R 02Y A.

SOC 02Y E Pretends social play with toys spontaneously
Credit is given if the client engages in simplified social play with puppets, stuffed animals, or dolls without supervision. Examples of social play include wrapping a blanket around a stuffed animal, placing a doll in bed, etc.

03 YEARS

SOC 03Y A Plays with peer unsupervised for 30 minutes
Credit is given if the client plays with a peer for a 30 minute period without need for supervision. Persons at this level are beginning to engage in cooperative play. Examples of social play activities include playing outside on gross motor equipment, building structures with blocks, listening to records, etc.

SOC 03Y B Waits turn in activities
Credit is given if the client awaits turn in activities when directed. Persons at this level respond to suggestions such as "wait, it's not your turn yet," or "it's your turn next."

SOC 03Y C Initiates conversations
Credit is given if the client initiates social conversations. Persons at this level carry on conversations with adults and peers without prompting.

SOC 03Y D Entertains less capable person
Credit is given if the client entertains a younger or less capable person for short periods. Persons at this level may take charge of a less capable or shy person at adult suggestion.

SOC 03Y E Participates in supervised group activity
Credit is given if the client participates in supervised cooperative group activities. Persons at this level engage in activities where reciprocal action is required. Examples of such activities include tea or birthday parties, playing house, ring-around-the-rosey, etc.

04 YEARS
SOC 04Y A Plays with peer for two hours
Credit is given if the client plays with peers for two hours without need for supervision. Persons at this level prefer social play to solitary play. Examples of social play activities range from the use of gross motor equipment to dramatic play.

SOC 04Y B Shares possessions
Credit is given if the client shares possessions with special friends on own initiative.

SOC 04Y C Converses socially during activities
Credit is given if the client combines social conversation with other activities such as dressing or eating.

SOC 04Y D Participates in show-and-tell activities
Credit is given if the client shows and tells about projects, possessions, own creations, and recent experiences in a descriptive manner.

SOC 04Y E Plays in loosely structured group game
Credit is given if the client participates in cooperative group activities which are loosely structured as to rules and leadership. Examples of activites include tag, hide-and-seek, and imaginative play such as cops-and-robbers.

05 YEARS

SOC 05Y A **Follows rules in supervised group games**
Credit is given if the client follows definite rules in supervised group games. Persons at this level participate in structured group games with adult leadership. Typical games played include musical chairs, hot-and-cold, animal charades, mother-may-I, Simon says, etc.

SOC 05Y B **Participates in group project**
Credit is given if the client engages in cooperative and purposeful group projects. Typical examples of group projects include activities such as constructing a toy city or sand castle and collecting items such as leaves or flowers.

SOC 05Y C **Practices social conventions with prompting**
Credit is given if the client practices social conventions with frequent reminders. Examples of typical expressions used at this level include asking for permission, "please," "thank you," "excuse me," etc.

SOC 05Y D **Helps care for less capable person**
Credit is given if the client shares care for a younger or less capable person. Persons at this level are able to assume limited responsibility for the care of another person. Typical care takes the form of "mother hen" type entertainment and protective supervision.

SOC 05Y E **Sings in group**
Credit is given if the client is able to join in song with others. Persons at this level are able to memorize simple words and melodies to songs. Songs learned are usually those taught at school, church, or home.

08 YEARS

SOC 08Y A **Participates in unsupervised group games**
Credit is given if the client participates in unsupervised neighborhood-type group play requiring loose rules. Typical group play at this level includes activities such as setting up a lemonade stand, playing baseball or football, going on hikes of bicycle rides, playing "horse," and building a fort or clubhouse.

SOC 08Y B Follows rules in group table games
Credit is given if the client participates in group table games following definite rules. Typical games played at this level include checkers, card games, yahtze, pick-up sticks, Chinese checkers, pool, ping pong, etc.

SOC 08Y C Practices social conventions without prompting
Credit is given if the client practices the common social conventions without reminders. Persons at this level are able to express proper greetings and farewells as well as other social proprieties such as ''thank you'' and ''you're welcome.''

SOC 08Y D Teaches less capable individual
Credit is given if the client teaches a younger or less capable person how to perform a simple task. Typical tasks taught at this level include rules of games, how to change a TV or radio station, how to operate an action toy, etc.

SOC 08Y E Dramatizes social situations
Credit is given if the client dramatizes social situations by role playing or through the medium of dolls or puppets.

12 YEARS

SOC 12Y A Participates as a team member
Credit is given if the client plays cooperatively in participant managed and organized group sports. Persons at this level participate in neighborhood-type team sports such as basketball, baseball, football, or volleyball. Rules and scoring techniques are understood and followed.

SOC 12Y B Participates in organized group activity
Credit is given if the client participates in organized clubs and activities such as scouts, 4-H, or class projects. Persons at this level are able to participate in structured group meetings following set formats and agendas and contribute to group projects.

SOC 12Y C Contributes to group discussion
Credit is given if the client participates in and contributes to group discussions with familiar persons. Persons at this level are clearly able to contribute to group discussions. Ability to contribute is evidenced

by being able to understand different points of view on a topic as well as taking a stand on an issue and explaining the reasons for the position chosen.

SOC 12Y D **Undertakes responsible child watching tasks**
Credit is given if the client demonstrates the skills and knowledge required for watching a younger or less capable person. Persons at this level are able to undertake child-watching tasks without supervision and are able to answer "What would you do if" questions regarding the sort of emergencies they need to be equipped to handle.

SOC 12Y E **Describes the qualities desired in a friend**
Credit is given if the client is able to describe the qualities looked for in a friend. Persons at this level are able to describe both the ideal characteristics of a friend as well as the characteristics of specific friends. Typical qualities described include loyalty, ability to keep secrets, easy to talk to, acceptance of others, dependability, similar interests, etc.

16 YEARS

SOC 16Y A **Plans, organizes, and excutes group activities**
Credit is given if the client is able to plan, organize, and execute various group activities or projects without need for adult supervision. Persons at this level are able to plan and carry out activities such as parties, picnics, or trips.

SOC 16Y B **Participates in special interest group**
Credit is given if the client participates in organized special interest groups. Persons at this level are able to identify personal interests and seek out groups which further enhance their knowledge or enjoyment of the particular interest, as well as increasing social contacts with people of similar interests. Examples of special interest groups include church youth groups, 4-H, youth political organizations, various school-associated clubs, etc.

SOC 16Y C **Demonstrates social courtesies without prompting**
Credit is given if the client is able to demonstrate social courtesies without prompting. Persons at this level are able to use or demonstrate the social courtesies common to social situations. Typical

courtesies demonstrated include introducing self or others, excusing self, receiving guests, etc.

SOC 16Y D **Demonstrates acceptable dating behavior**
Credit is given if the client demonstrates acceptable dating behavior without supervision. Persons at this level agree upon mutually acceptable activity, arrive or are ready at the expected time, adhere to curfew requirements, determine financial arrangements in advance, etc.

SOC 16Y E **Reacts to novel social setting appropriately**
Credit is given if the client describes or demonstrates appropriate reactions to unusual social situations. Persons at this level are able to describe appropriate reactions to situations involving embarassment or danger to self or others. Typical hypothetical situations include spilling something in a restaurant, finding self without adequate funds on a date, driving and being offered an alcoholic drink by friends, etc.

ORIENTATION

03 MONTHS

ORI 03M A **Investigates self or objects**
Credit is given if the client explores self and the external environment. Persons at this level are becoming aware of themselves and objects within reach. Examples of exploration include feeling, mouthing, or looking at their own fingers and exploring their own face, eyes, and mouth with their hand.

ORI 03M B **Anticipates routine happenings**
Credit is given if the client is observed to anticipate routine happenings as evidenced by changing posture or body activity. Persons at this level increase activity or tense body when approached for feeding or to be picked up, etc.

ORI 03M C **Follows vanishing object with head**
Credit is given if the client follows a vanishing object with head. Persons at this level follow a slowly moving object with eyes and head and look for a vanishing object very briefly by turning head when the object moves out of peripheral vision.

ORI 03M D **Discriminates novel from routine experiences**
Credit is given if the client is observed to discriminate novel from routine experiences as evidenced by changing posture, body activity, or facial experession. Persons at this level respond to novel stimuli with such changes in behavior as a startle response, looking around wide-eyed, waving arms and kicking legs, etc.

ORI 03M E **Searches with eyes for sound**
Credit is given if the client searches with eyes for the source of a sound. Persons at this level look in the direction of a sound and may glance from one object to another in response to the sound of each.

06 MONTHS

ORI 06M A   **Responds positively to own mirror image**

Credit is given if the client smiles, vocalizes, pats, fingers, regards, mouths, or reaches toward own image in a mirror.

ORI 06M B   **Anticipates routine happenings**

Credit is given if the client smiles, reaches out, or becomes excited when approached for routines such as bathing, feeding, playing, etc. This item is differentiated from ORI 03M B by the clarity of the anticipatory responses. Responses at the three month level are more subtle and require more interpretation by the observer.

ORI 06M C   **Searches for vanishing object**

Credit is given if the client follows a vanishing object with head. Persons at this level follow a slowly moving object with eyes and head and search for a vanishing object for short periods of time. The search continues even if the item has moved out of sight such as when an object falls off a table onto the floor but can be seen by looking downward. Persons at this level sometimes make a game out of dropping objects in order to view the objects and then protest or call to others to return the dropped items.

ORI 06M D   **Discriminates unfamiliar person**

Credit is given if the client discriminates between familiar and unfamiliar people. Persons at this level approach, withdraw, or otherwise plainly respond differentially to the presence and attention of familiar and unfamiliar people.

ORI 06M E   **Explores objects**

Credit is given if the client experiments with the properties of objects. Persons at this level touch, look at, rattle, turn, crackle, bend or roll such things as paper, food, squeeze toys, etc.

12 MONTHS

ORI 12M A   **Knows own name**

Credit is given if the client knows own name as evidenced by coming when called, looking around when name is called, etc.

ORI 12M B   Differentiates between objects
Credit is given if the client differentiates between objects. Persons at this level are able to pick up a named object from an assortment of two or three familiar objects or exhibit a preference when given a choice of several objects.

ORI 12M C   Retrieves hidden object
Credit is given if the client retrieves an object that is seen hidden. Persons at this level are able to find objects that are hidden close-at-hand and in a conspicuous manner. Examples include retrieving an object seen hidden in a covered container by removing the covering or retrieving an object seen hidden under a cloth or paper covering by removing the covering.

ORI 12M D   Plays orientation games
Credit is given if the client is able to learn and play orientation games such as up-and-down-with-arms, how-big-is-the-baby, where-is-the-baby, etc.

ORI 12M E   Differentiates between familiar persons
Credit is given if the client differentiates between familiar people. Persons at this level evidence this ability by handing an object differentially to one of two familiar persons when one is named or pointed to, or by looking in the direction of a named person, etc.

18 MONTHS

ORI 18M A   Points to named body parts
Credit is given if the client points to own anatomy or parts of a doll on request. Persons at this level are able to point to principal body parts such as eye, nose, hair, mouth, or ear.

ORI 18M B   Associates future events with routines
Credit is given if the client understands that certain activities follow other activities as a matter of daily routine. Persons at this level understand time relationships such as playing with toys after breakfast, taking a nap after lunch, and taking a bath after dinner.

ORI 18M C   Shows where familiar things are kept
Credit is given if the client indicates where familiar

possessions are kept when requested. Persons at this level show where things are kept by going to the place of storage, by fetching or returning items to the place of storage, etc.

ORI 18M D   **Follows two of four orientation directions**
Credit is given if the client follows two of four directions with ball or other easily held toy. Persons at this level are able to follow two of the following four directions: (1) "Take the ball to _____" (2) "Put the ball on the table" (3) "Bring the ball to me" (4) "Put the ball on the chair."

ORI 18M E   **Says or gestures goodbye**
Credit is given if the client gestures or verbalizes farewells with termination as the meaning. Persons at this level wave or say "bye-bye" unprompted, in response to adult prompting, or in response to farewells communicated by others.

02 YEARS

ORI 02Y A   **Refers to self and family by name**
Credit is given if the client refers to self and members of immediate family by name. Persons at this level are able to identify self and family members in a mirror or picture or in person. Identification is made by giving appropriate labels such as "me" or "mommy."

ORI 02Y B   **Knows words denoting the future**
Credit is given if the client uses or responds to words denoting the future. Examples of words used or responded to include "gonna," "in a minute," "wait," "pretty soon," etc.

ORI 02Y C   **Identifies possessions of family members**
Credit is given if the client identifies familiar possessions of members of immediate family and indicates to whom they belong. Objects identified include items such as coat, shoe, or bed. Indication of ownership can take the form of naming the owner, pointing to the owner or picture of the owner, or by taking the item to the owner.

ORI 02Y D   **Follows four of four orientation directions**
Credit is given if the client follows four of four direc-

tions with a ball or other easily held toy. For a description of the four directions followed, see ORI 18M D.

ORI 02Y E **Knows words denoting the present**
Credit is given if the client uses or responds to words denoting the present time. Examples or words used or responded to include "now," "today," "this day," etc.

03 YEARS

ORI 03Y A **Gives first and last name, and sex**
Credit is given if the client is able to give first and last name, and sex when questioned. Persons at this level are able to respond appropriately to questions such as "Are you a boy or a girl?" or "What is your first name?"

ORI 03Y B **Matches objects by shape or color**
Credit is given if the client matches familiar like objects by grouping them as to color or form. Persons at this level are able to match objects by sorting into piles or groups of the same color or shape. Typical shapes matched are circles, triangles, squares, etc. Typical colors matched include the primary colors of red, green, blue, and yellow.

ORI 03Y C **Compares size of objects**
Credit is given if the client compares the size of two obviously different sized objects of the same shape. Persons at this level are able to respond correctly to questions and commands such as "Which is bigger?"; " Show me the big one."; "Which is longer?"; "Show me the long one."

ORI 03Y D **Follows directions containing prepositions**
Credit is given if the client responds correctly to commissions containing prepositions indicating the position of an object relative to other objects. Persons at this level are able to follow directions containing prepositions such as in, on, and under. An example of a typical commission is "Put the ball under the chair."

ORI 03Y E **Answers simple orientation questions**
Credit is given if the client is able to answer simple questions related to person, time, or place. Persons

at this level are able to answer questions such as "How old are you?"; "When do you go to bed?"; "Where do you live?"

04 YEARS

ORI 04Y A   **Names several colors**
Credit is given if the client is able to name five or more colors. Persons at this level are able to identify basic colors such as red, white, blue, green, black, yellow, orange, or brown.

ORI 04Y B   **Knows when events take place**
Credit is given if the client demonstrates a reasonably clear understanding of when events of the day take place in relation to each other. Persons at this level are able to demonstrate this skill by answering questions such as "What do you do after you get up?" or "What do you do before you eat lunch?"

ORI 04Y C   **Compares objects by weight and texture**
Credit is given if the client is able to compare the weight or texture of objects by selecting the correct item in response to a cue. Persons at this level are able to respond correctly to questions and commands such as "Which is heavier?"; "Show me the heavy one."; "Which is smoother?"; " Show me the smooth one."

ORI 04Y D   **Performs commissions containing prepositions**
Credit is given if the client responds correctly to commissions containing prepositions indicating the position of an object. Persons at this level are able to follow directions containing prepositions such as in front of, behind, beside, or on top of. An example of a typical commission is "Put the chair beside the table."

ORI 04Y E   **Knows living location**
Credit is given if the client answers two out of four of the following orientation questions: (1) "What is the color of your house?" (2) "What street do you live on?" (3) "Who lives in the house next to yours?" (4) What town do you live in or near?"

05 YEARS

ORI 05Y A   **Draws picture of person**
Credit is given if the client draws an unmistakable picture of a person. Persons at this level are able to

draw a picture of a person which includes the basic body parts: trunk, arms, legs, feet, mouth, nose, eyes, etc.

ORI 05Y B **Gives opposites**
Credit is given if the client answers simple opposite analogy questions (e.g., Walking is slow, running is __ ; Elephants are big, ants are __ ; etc.) and gives opposites for orientation words such as few, forward, backward, tiny, smooth, or high.

ORI 05Y C **Distinguishes own right from left hand**
Credit is given if the client distinguishes left and right hand on own person but not necessarily on other persons. This skill is usually tested simply by asking the person to show their left or right hand.

ORI 05Y D **Knows how to get to familiar locations**
Credit is given if the client is able to demonstrate knowledge of the route to familiar locations within a several mile radius. Persons at this level are able to indicate how to get to familiar locations by going there on request, showing the way, or by describing the route.

ORI 05Y E **Knows age and days of the week**
Credit is given if the client answers three out of four of the following orientation questions: (1) "How old will you be on your next birthday?" (2) "What day is today?" (3) "What day comes after Sunday?" (4) "What are the names of all the days in the week?"

08 Years
ORI 08Y A **Compares self to others**
Credit is given if the client demonstrates an awareness of similarities and differences between people. Persons at this level are able to list ways that he or she is similar or different from other persons. Examples of characteristics commonly listed include skin, eye, or hair color; wearing of glasses; and ability in school/play activities.

ORI 08Y B **Knows personal time schedule**
Credit is given if the client demonstrates an awareness of his or her personal time schedule. Persons at this level are able to answer questions regarding the occurrence of events during the course of

the day. Examples of questions answered include: "What time do you get up in the morning?"; "When do you go to school?"; "What time do you eat lunch?"; "When do you get home from school?"; etc. This level person is also able to consult a bulletin board about his or her schedule concerning activities such as those at school or camp.

ORI 08Y C   **Understands basic conservation concepts**
Credit is given if the client performs two out of three cognitive tasks which assess conservational (Piagetian) concepts about substance (amount), length, and number. Persons at this level are able to demonstrate an understanding of the following concepts: (1) The amount of a substance (e.g., clay or water) doesn't change when its shape is altered, (2) The length of a line/string doesn't change when its position relative to another line/string of equal length is altered or when the shape of the line/string is altered, and (3) The number of a group of items doesn't change when the spatial arrangement of the items is changed.

ORI 08Y D   **Locates landmarks on a simplified map**
Credit is given if the client is able to locate landmarks such as roads, rivers, schools, or stores on a simplified map. Persons at this level are able to draw a map of their immediate neighborhood and are able to compare locations on a simplified map as to relative distance and direction.

ORI 08Y E   **Knows time, months, year and season**
Credit is given if the client answers three out of four of the following orientation questions: (1) "What time is it according to that clock?" (2) "What are the names of all the months?" (3) "What season is it?" (4) "What is today's date?" Either the day, month, or year is an adequate answer to the last question.

12 YEARS
ORI 12Y A   **Knows own assets and shortcomings**
Credit is given if the client is able to realistically describe own personal assets and shortcomings. Examples of behavioral characteristics mentioned in such self-evaluations include: "I chew my nails"; "I usually remember birthdays"; "I fight with my sister"; "Sometimes I don't do what I'm told to do."; etc.

ORI 12Y B **Draws a floor plan of own home**
Credit is given if the client draws a floor plan of his or her own home. Persons at this level are able to draw a reasonably accurate schematic which indicates the relative location of rooms, doors, windows, etc.

ORI 12Y C **Names extended family**
Credit is given if the client names extended family members and tells where they live. Persons at this level are able to name grandparents, aunts and uncles, cousins, etc. and tell where they live.

ORI 12Y D **Locates state, town, and home on map**
Credit is given if the client is able to use maps to locate his or her state, town, and home.

ORI 12Y E **Defines abstract orientation concepts**
Credit is given if the client is able to adequately define concepts such as time, space, love, self, death, etc. Examples of satisfactory definitions include: "Time is how long things take."; "Space is something empty."; "Self is all of me."; etc.

16 YEARS

ORI 16Y A **Knows own potential**
Credit is given if the client assesses and describes own academic or job potential. Persons at this level are able to assess their own strengths and weaknesses relative to educational and career planning. Assessments at this level may be overly optimistic but should be within the realm of possibility given the client's interests and demonstrated ability.

ORI 16Y B **Outlines plan for the future**
Credit is given if the client outlines a four year plan covering education, work, and personal living. Planning at this level may be overly optimistic regarding future expectations but should be within the realm of possibility given the current situation and demonstrated ability of the client.

ORI 16Y C **Estimates distance, heights, etc.**
Credit is given if the client gives reasonable estimations of distance, heights, weights, ages, amounts, etc. Persons at this level are able to give accurate estimations such as the distance from home to

school, the height of a tree in the backyard, the weight and age of strangers, and the amount of gas left in the car.

ORI 16Y D **Locates address**

Credit is given if the client is able to locate a specific address using a city map. Persons at this level are able to obtain an address using a phone book, locate that address on a map, and then drive or direct a driver to that specific location using a logical route.

ORI 16Y E **Plans a trip**

Credit is given if the client prepares a plan for an interstate car trip including route, stop points, and projected times between points.

SELF-DIRECTION

03 MONTHS

S-D 03M A **Stops activity to listen to a sound**
Credit is given if the client stops an activity to listen to a sound. Persons at this level will stop what they are doing to listen to the sound of a voice and will turn their head toward or search with their eyes for the source of a sound.

S-D 03M B **Quiets with change of scene**
Credit is given if the client quiets when given a change of scene. Persons at this level typically quiet when upset when given distractions. Typical distractions include propping or holding into a sitting position, taking from the immediate area, or showing interesting toys.

S-D 03M C **Repeats behavior which produces a change**
Credit is given if the client repeats a physical activity or vocalization which produces an observable effect on the environment. Examples include vocalizations that result in adult attention, kicking feet or batting with arms when the result is movement of an overhead mobile, etc. Such environmental responses to a person's actions are especially important since the discovery of such predictable responses are the basis for volitional behavior and awareness of cause-and-effect relationships.

S-D 03M D **Blinks at object near eyes**
Credit is given if the client blinks when an object such as a hand passes across the field of vision close to the eyes.

S-D 03M E **Quiets when attended**
Credit is given if the client quiets when given special attention. Persons at this level respond positively to attention such as being held or rocked, being given a back rub, or being given a bath.

06 MONTHS

S-D 06M A Removes tissue placed on face
Credit is given if the client removes light coverings placed over face. Persons at this level remove coverings such as tissue paper or a small cloth placed on the face. Coverings are usually removed by actions such as moving the head back-and-forth or swiping with a hand or arm.

S-D 06M B Stops fussing when distracted with toy or music
Credit is given if the client's behavior is modified in a positive direction when given a small toy or other interesting object or when music is played. When experiencing minor upset, persons at this level stop crying or fussing when presented with distracting stimuli such as small toys or music.

S-D 06M C Repeats behavior which is imitated
Credit is given if the client repeats a specific behavior which is imitated by another person. At this level, the trainer imitates a specific behavior pattern of the client. The client, in turn, repeats the imitated behavior. Typical behaviors imitated include sounds, facial expressions, and manipulations of objects such as toys.

S-D 06M D Attends to subtle stimuli
Credit is given if the client attends briefly to subtle stimuli. Persons at this level attend to subtle stimuli such as a scribbling demonstration, small edible objects such as an M&M candy, and low volume music or sound. Attention is typically very brief and may only amount to a glance or other attending response for one or two seconds.

S-D 06M E Inhibits behavior briefly after being stopped
Credit is given if the client inhibits an undesirable behavior after being stopped. Persons at this level will stop undesirable behaviors - such as throwing food or utensils on the floor - when physically stopped from doing so. Inhibition usually lasts only a brief period of time.

12 MONTHS

S-D 12M A Responds to social reward
Credit is given if the client performs behaviors that

are socially rewarded. Persons at this level initiate, repeat, or imitate behaviors which are socially reinforced by another person. Examples of social rewards given at this level include praise, smiles, pats, laughter, and exaggerated surprise.

S-D 12M B **Inhibits briefly when told no**
Credit is given if the client stops current activity for a brief period of time when given a cue such as "no." Persons at this level are beginning to respond to inhibitory cues, but responses are short-lived and level of understanding is rudimentary.

S-D 12M C **Performs new movements after being assisted**
Credit is given if the client performs new movements after manually helped to make the movements. Persons at this level are beginning to imitate but learn best when demonstration is accompanied by physical assistance in performing new actions.

S-D 12M D **Attends to novel stimulus**
Credit is given if the client attends to a variety of novel stimuli for short periods of time. Persons at this level attend to such novel experiences as toys which make interesting sounds and movements when manipulated, or a projected picture of a person. The length of attention may be as short as 5 seconds for a picture or much longer for interesting toys.

S-D 12M E **Cooperates with simple requests**
Credit is given if the client cooperates with simple requests such as "Come here," or "Give that to me." Persons at this level respond to a few simple directions such as giving up a toy upon request, but such responses are highly inconsistent.

18 MONTHS

S-D 18M A **Changes activities cooperatively if prompted**
Credit is given if the client switches from one activity to another without resistance if a game is made out of the transition. Examples of transition techniques include luring from one room to another with a toy or edible treat, chasing or being chased, hiding, etc.

S-D 18M B **Stops or delays activity when given special cues**
Credit is given if the client accepts termination of situations by being told, "thank you" or "bye-bye"

and can be put off by being told "after_____."

S-D 18M C   Imitates newly observed actions
Credit is given if the client imitates actions never before performed. Persons at this level perform new actions such as retrieving out-of-reach objects with a stick, making walking motions with a block, rolling or tossing a ball toward another person, attempting to kick a ball, turning pages of a book, turning knobs on a toy radio, putting shapes into a shape sorting container, and blowing out matches or candles.

S-D 18M D   Establishes eye contact when called
Credit is given if the client interrupts an on-going activity and establishes eye contact when name is called.

S-D 18M E   Demonstrates beginning awareness of hazards
Credit is given if the client demonstrates a beginning awareness of unsafe objects or situations. Persons at this level avoid or practice caution around unsafe objects such as burning material, animal excrement, or broken glass and may use expressions or signs to label objects or situations to be avoided.

02 YEARS
S-D 02Y A   Goes about area briefly unattended
Credit is given if the client goes about the home or yard unattended. Persons at this level are able to be left for brief periods in familiar and "safe" surroundings without getting into or causing serious problems. The yard may need to be fenced for the client to be left alone, and he or she needs to be checked every 5 or 10 minutes.

S-D 02Y B   Responds to a variety of inhibitory cues
Credit is given if the client inhibits behavior when given cues such as "stop," "come here," "no," "when it's time," "wait," "in a minute," or "pretty soon." Typically, a redirection cue accompanies the inhibitory cue. Examples of redirection cues include "sit down," "watch TV," "go to your room," "go outside," "play with your brother," etc.

S-D 02Y C   Imitates peer behavior when cued
Credit is given if the client is able to imitate peer behavior when prompted. Persons at this level re-

spond to cues such as "look at what _____ is doing; let's see if you can do that." Peer behavior can be used as a model for learning skills as well as a model for cooperation and good behavior.

S-D 02Y D   **Demonstrates preference for specific items**
Credit is given if the client demonstrates a preference for specific foods, clothes, toys, etc. Persons at this level demonstrate preferences by pointing to, picking up, or naming desired objects.

S-D 02Y E   **Shares toy when told**
Credit is given if the client shares a toy or other possession for a brief period at adult suggestion. Persons at this level may have a difficult time sharing a toy that they are playing with, but usually can be talked into giving up another toy that they are not playing with at the moment.

03 YEARS

S-D 03Y A   **Works for praise**
Credit is given if the client values social reinforcement and performs tasks for rewards such as praise and pats. Persons at this level perform new tasks or repeat accomplishments when told, "good boy/girl," "nice job," etc. Social reinforcement may also take the form of a pat on the back or a hug.

S-D 03Y B   **Tolerates delays with promise of later**
Credit is given if the client tolerates short delays by promise of later. Persons at this level can be put off with promise of later or after____. For example, "After lunch you can have a cookie," "After your nap you can go out and play," etc.

S-D 03Y C   **Performs non-preferred tasks given a reason**
Credit is given if the client performs non-preferred tasks if given a good reason including step-by-step suggestion (e.g., "Let's pick up the blocks so we have room to play. First, we pick up the big blocks and then_____.")

S-D 03Y D   **Relaxes for 10 minutes during story or music**
Credit is given if the client remains quiet while listening to a story or music. Persons at this level are able to relax for 10-15 minutes while sitting or lying on a mat or blanket during a quiet time activity.

S-D 03Y E　**Improves own behavior after group removal**
Credit is given if the client modifies own behavior in a positive manner after removal from a group activity. Persons at this level modify own behavior in order to regain a preferred activity or a lost privilege.

04 YEARS

S-D 04Y A　**Follows rules regarding boundaries**
Credit is given if the client follows rules regarding limits on how far he or she can range from the home or other location. Persons at this level are able to understand and follow simple rules such as staying in a particular area in the house, staying in the yard, staying on the sidewalk and out of the street, or waiting for an adult at a crosswalk. Rules are understood and followed, but frequent checking is necessary because of susceptibility to distractions.

S-D 04Y B　**Works for extension of privileges**
Credit is given if the client is motivated to perform simple chores in anticipation of a special reward. Persons at this level respond to contingencies such as "If you pick up your toys, then you can watch an extra half-hour of TV;" or "If you put the dishes in the sink, then you can go to a friend's house."

S-D 04Y C　**Improves behavior as a result of redirection**
Credit is given if the client improves inappropriate behavior when an appropriate substitute activity is suggested. Persons at this level respond to verbal redirection. Examples of redirection include suggesting activities such as a walk or coloring pictures to curb racing around or pushing, suggesting a new topic to discourage silly conversation, etc.

S-D 04Y D　**Demonstrates knowledge of unpleasant consequences**
Credit is given if the client demonstrates an awareness that misconduct and other forbidden behaviors can result in unpleasant consequences. Awareness is evidenced by words or actions. Examples of types of consequences understood include restriction or other punishments for acts such as fighting or leaving without permission, injury as a possible consequence for playing in the street or playing with fire, etc.

S-D 04Y E   **Asks permission for privileges**
Credit is given if the client follows household rules regarding gaining permission before engaging in special privileges. Persons at this level ask permission for privileges such as fixing self a snack, visiting a nearby friend, or playing with restricted toys.

05 YEARS

S-D 05Y A   **Changes activity with advanced warning**
Credit is given if the client changes from one activity to another given advanced notice. Persons at this level respond to warnings or directions such as "Get ready for bed as soon as the TV show is over," "We're leaving in just a few minutes," or "Put your toys away."

S-D 05Y B   **Follows kindergarten rules**
Credit is given if the client understands and follows rules characteristic of kindergarten level situations. Examples of kindergarten-type rules include going directly to home or school, taking turns, cleaning up after activities, asking for permission, being quiet when another person is talking, using crosswalks, obeying traffic signals, staying in the immediate neighborhood, etc.

S-D 05Y C   **Communicates that lying and theft are wrong**
Credit is given if the client demonstrates knowledge that lying is telling untruths, stealing is taking things that belong to others, and that both acts are forbidden. Knowledge is evidenced by verbal response to questions or by past history.

S-D 05Y D   **Hastens when told to hurry**
Credit is given if the client performs faster when told to hurry.

S-D 05Y E   **Indicates own ability with some accuracy**
Credit is given if the client demonstrates knowledge of own ability to perform familiar tasks. Persons at this level have a fairly realistic understanding of their own ability and can answer "can you" questions with reasonable accuracy.

08 YEARS

S-D 08Y A   **Demonstrates ability to empathize**
Credit is given if the client correctly answers questions as to how another person would or ought to feel under various unpleasant circumstances. Types of

feelings described include those experienced when a person is falsely accused, called names, punished, teased, loses a pet, etc.

S-D 08Y B   Modifies own behavior following deprivation
Credit is given if the client modifies own behavior when the consequence is a specific deprivation. Persons at this level improve their behavior as a result of loss or threat of loss of privileges such as watching a favorite TV show, staying up late, or receiving an allowance.

S-D 08Y C   Lists rules in home, school, or community
Credit is given if the client is able to list some of the common rules of propriety in everyday interpersonal interaction. Examples of rules described include being a good sport, giving everyone a turn, not making fun of people, not starting fights, going along with the majority, etc.

S-D 08Y D   Improves behavior while on token system
Credit is given if the client improves or maintains level of performance if provided with a chart or list of assigned chores or tasks and a system for reward with money, privileges, or other compensation. Persons at this level commonly earn an allowance for performance at home or school. Systems for compensation may be informal or may consist of a point system which allows for degrees of reward and compensation.

S-D 08Y E   Corrects actions after viewing mistakes of others
Credit is given if the client corrects own behavior in response to observing the mistakes of others and the consequences of the mistakes. Persons at this level are able to learn lessons by observing the consequences of others' actions at home, school, or in the community.

12 YEARS
S-D 12Y A   Describes effects of stress on own behavior
Credit is given if the client describes how changes in physical or emotional state affect one's behavior. Persons at this level are able to describe how behavior worsens when one is tired, ill, or upset and how behavior improves when one feels especially well.

S-D 12Y B   **Controls own emotional behavior**
Credit is given if the client controls own emotional behavior. Persons at this level are usually able to keep verbal and physical impulses in check when angered. Typical responses and outlets for anger include silence, walking away, seeking solitude, laughing it off, engaging in physical exercise, counting to self, etc.

S-D 12Y C   **Describes various ethical standards**
Credit is given if the client contributes to group discussion of issues concerning ethical conduct relative to various situations. Persons at this level are able to discuss issues such as "Robin Hood" conduct, the "Golden Rule," white lies, or "an eye-for-an-eye" concept of punishment.

S-D 12Y D   **Weighs the pros and cons of decisions**
Credit is given if the client demonstrates an ability to resolve conflicts by analyzing the pros and cons of opposing decisions or actions. Persons at this level are able to weigh the positive and negative aspects of one or more alternatives to arrive at the final decision.

S-D 12Y E   **Persuades others without using force**
Credit is given if the client uses persuasion rather than force as a method for changing the behavior of others. Persons at this level typically use rational argument or negotiation to persuade others rather than verbal or physical intimidation and threats.

16 YEARS
S-D 16Y A   **Describes forces which control own behavior**
Credit is given if the client is able to describe some of the forces which help people keep their own behavior and impulses under control. Persons at this level give answers which include statements about forces such as parents, conscience, personal ethics, morals, religious convictions, and fear or respect for the law or other higher authority.

S-D 16Y B   **Describes effective self-improvement system**
Credit is given if the client is able to describe systems which are effective in modifying a behavior or characteristic in one's self. Persons at this level

include in their description ideas such as analysis of causative factors, self-observation, contracts with self, self-reinforcement, or arrangements with others for rewards or reminders. Examples of behaviors needing improvement include lack of self-confidence, obesity, chewing nails, poor study habits, etc.

S-D 16Y C   **Analyzes controversial moral issues**
Credit is given if the client is able to analyze controversial moral issues. Persons at this level are able to describe the pros and cons of issues such as euthanasia, abortion, illegal drugs, alcohol, promiscuity, pornography, or capital punishment.

S-D 16Y D   **Analyzes effects of action on self and others**
Credit is given if the client is able to describe how various decisions affect self and others on both a short and long term basis. Examples of decisions with important consequences include spending money, accepting a job, going steady, moving to a new community, stealing, lying, etc.

S-D 16Y E   **Describes legal consequences of various acts**
Credit is given if the client is able to answer questions concerning the legal consequences of a variety of situations. Persons at this level are able to describe the legal consequences of situations such as sexual conduct, crime against persons and property, contractual agreements, felonies versus misdemeanors, or constitutional rights.

INTERPRETING AND USING THE RESULTS

The uses of Grid adaptive behavior assessments include (1) the identification of training needs for individual clients, (2) the determination of change in skill levels over time for individual clients, (3) the statistical description of groups of clients, and (4) the classification of individual clients. Each of the first three uses will be discussed briefly. Classification will be discussed in some detail.

Identification of Training Needs

The results of Grid assessments can be used for the identification of training needs for individual clients. For example, the ten skill cluster scores can be compared for relative strengths and weaknesses. Special attention for training can then be given to the skill clusters having the lowest scores. In addition, each skill cluster can be examined for the lowest items which have been failed. These items are the logical targets for focus in training programs. This follows the idea of "filling in the gaps" that was described in the INTRODUCTION. Once specific needs are identified by examining the gaps in the Grid, then training objectives can be written and training activities developed using accepted educational methodology.

The specific items comprising the strengths and weaknesses for a Grid assessment can be identified by using one of several objective methods:

1. The relative strengths and weaknesses are the highest two credited items and the lowest two uncredited items in each skill cluster.
2. The relative strengths and weaknesses are the highest two credited items in each of the highest five skill clusters and the lowest two uncredited items in each of the five lowest skill clusters.
3. The relative strengths and weaknesses are the highest ten credited items and the lowest ten uncredited items in the Grid.
4. The relative strengths and weaknesses are all of the credited items in the top two levels of the Grid and all of the uncredited items in the bottom two levels having uncredited items.

5. The standard deviation is calculated for the Grid assessment, and the relative strengths and weaknesses are those items that are above and below one standard deviation from the ADL.

Determination of Change

A Grid assessment yields an overall developmental score (ADL) as well as individual skill cluster scores. These scores can be compared with the same scores on previous or subsequent asessments. Such comparisons provide information as to the client's progress, maintenance, or regression in skill levels. This information, in turn, reflects the adequacy of the client's current situation and related need for change.

Statistical Description

Grid scores can be used for a variety of statistical purposes. The following examples represent some of the many statistical applications:

1. The population of a treatment facility can be described by the mean ADL and skill cluster scores. In addition, the range and standard deviation can be determined for further description.

2. The number of clients in each of several Grid developmental age ranges can be determined. This type of information can be more useful than merely knowing the number of clients in each of the adaptive behavior classifications, since each of the classifications covers a rather broad developmental range.

3. The lowest and highest skill clusters can be determined for a group of clients. Such information can be used to help determine program priorities.

4. Grid scores can be used as criteria for grouping clients into training programs or living areas.

Classification

Although there are a number of instruments for assessing adaptive behavior, there are no generally accepted procedures for using the information from one or more of these scales to classify residents in terms of their adaptive behavior. The guidelines contained in the 1959 AAMD classification manual were vague. The newer 1973, 1977, and 1983 manuals from the AAMD contain much more illustrative material, however, the classification problem is no closer to solution. In the later manual, the task of classification is assigned to the use of standardized scales supplemented by clinical judgement. Details as to how to accomplish this task are not further specified.

Because of this problem of making systematic and objective judgements regarding the classification of mentally retarded persons, the following assumptions and procedures were developed:

1. Every individual may be evaluated with respect to his or her performance on a scale listing the behaviors expected from people-in-general at different specified ages. The Grid is such a scale, as is the original Vineland Social Maturity Scale. These two scales, as well as others similarly constructed, yield a single index to describe the developmental age level of persons rated on the scales. The Vineland provides a social age (SA) and the Grid yields an average developmental level (ADL). A method for classification using the developmental age from a scale such as the Grid is described as follows:

2. The person whose developmental age (DA) is equivalent to his chronological age is performing at an expected level of adaptive behavior. Figure 1 contains a set of curves showing the relationship between DA and CA for selected ratios. For example, the uppermost curve shows a relationship where DA=CA, the next curve shows a relationship where DA=.85CA, the next DA=.70CA, etc. The selected ratios illustrated in Figure 1 were chosen because they are similar to those that describe levels of retardation as defined by measured intelligence. Consistent with the practice followed in classifying persons in terms of measured intelligence, the .70 level is used to distinguish between the not retarded and mildly retarded levels of adaptive behavior. The ranges of ratios used to define the four classes or retarded adaptive behavior are .69 to .55 for mild, .40 to .54 for moderate, .25 to .39 for severe, and .24 and below for profound (see Figure 1).

3. Table 2 is derived from Figure 1 and shows the ranges of DA for CA's from 5.0 to 16.0. The ranges are listed for the classes of adaptive behavior. The table can be used to classify a client when his DA and CA are known. Entering the table on the row corresponding to the CA, the column containing the DA range can be found. The heading of the column above the DA range shows the adaptive behavior class for the client.

4. There is an area of confusion about how to handle the classification of persons who are adults. Since this classification system utilizes a ratio in which CA is the denominator, a client's classification can become lower merely because the resident increases in age. The use of a ratio makes sense during the period when adaptive behavior is increasing along with age, but when development slows or stops and age continues to increase, the illusion of adaptive behavior deteriation is not accurate. This problem can be solved by setting an age limit beyond which CA as a denominator is not increased. The authors of the Grid have chosen 16.0 years as this age limit. The age limit was chosen based upon the authors' experience in searching the literature for descriptions of normal age-graded skills. By 16 years of age, normal individuals have the skills required for independent living. Beyond this age, further development is primarily a matter of opportunity for applying the skills already present and further education. This view is supported by the writings of David Wechsler who chose 16 as the age when mental development is essentially complete. For these reasons, the 16.0 year limit is substituted for the actual CA of a client when his or her actual age is greater than 16.0. This rule applies in using Table 2 for classifying clients in terms of their adaptive behavior.

Given a client's CA and ADL, Table 2 can be employed to arrive at an objective adaptive behavior classification. However, only a trained professional should interpret the results and make the final decision as to the classification. Special circumstances or handicapping conditions can justify the modification of an objectively determined classification. As stated in the 1983 AAMD classification manual, "In the final analysis, clinical judgement is needed to arrive at an estimate of adaptive behavior." For an examination of the validity of this classification procedure, see the STANDARDIZATION section of this manual.

Figure 1

RELATIONSHIP BETWEEN DA AND CA
FOR DIFFERENT CLASSES OF ADAPTIVE BEHAVIOR

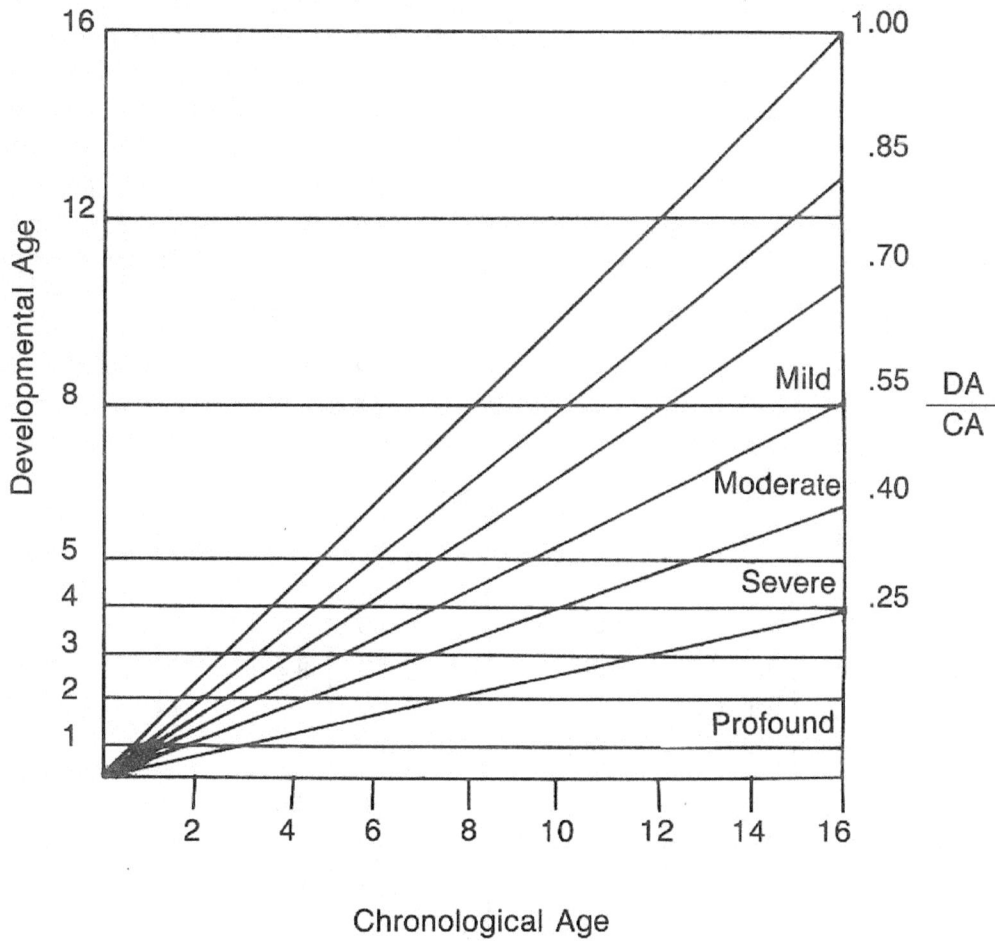

Table 2
DEVELOPMENTAL AGES FOR CLASSES OF ADAPTIVE BEHAVIOR

Chrono. Age	SEVERITY OF RETARDATION										Chrono. Age
	Profound		Severe		Moderate		Mild		Not Retarded		
	From	To	From	To	From	To	From	To	From	To	
5.0-5.4	--	1.2	1.3	1.9	2.0	2.7	2.8	3.4	3.5	--	5.0-5.4
5.5-5.9	--	1.3	1.4	2.1	2.2	2.9	3.0	3.9	4.0	--	5.5-5.9
6.0-6.4	--	1.4	1.5	2.3	2.4	3.2	3.3	4.1	4.2	--	6.0-6.4
6.5-6.9	--	1.5	1.6	2.5	2.6	3.5	3.6	4.5	4.6	--	6.5-6.9
7.0-7.4	--	1.7	1.8	2.7	2.8	3.8	3.9	4.8	4.9	--	7.0-7.4
7.5-7.9	--	1.8	1.9	2.9	3.0	4.0	4.1	5.2	5.3	--	7.5-7.9
8.0-8.4	--	1.9	2.0	3.1	3.2	4.3	4.4	5.5	5.6	--	8.0-8.4
8.5-8.9	--	2.0	2.1	3.3	3.4	4.6	4.7	5.9	6.0	--	8.5-8.9
9.0-9.4	--	2.2	2.3	3.5	3.6	4.9	5.0	6.2	6.3	--	9.0-9.4
9.5-9.9	--	2.3	2.4	3.7	3.8	5.1	5.2	6.6	6.7	--	9.5-9.9
10.0-10.4	--	2.4	2.5	3.9	4.0	5.4	5.5	6.9	7.0	--	10.0-10.4
10.5-10.9	--	2.5	2.6	4.1	4.2	5.7	5.8	7.3	7.4	--	10.5-10.9
11.0-11.4	--	2.7	2.8	4.3	4.4	6.0	6.1	7.6	7.7	--	11.0-11.4
11.5-11.9	--	2.8	2.9	4.5	4.6	6.2	6.3	8.0	8.1	--	11.5-11.9
12.0-12.4	--	2.9	3.0	4.7	4.8	6.5	6.6	8.3	8.4	--	12.0-12.4
12.5-12.9	--	3.0	3.1	4.9	5.0	6.8	6.9	8.7	8.8	--	12.5-12.9
13.0-13.4	--	3.2	3.3	5.1	5.2	7.1	7.2	9.1	9.2	--	13.0-13.4
13.5-13.9	--	3.3	3.4	5.3	5.4	7.3	7.4	9.4	9.5	--	13.5-13.9
14.0-14.4	--	3.4	3.5	5.5	5.6	7.6	7.7	9.7	9.8	--	14.0-14.4
14.5-14.9	--	3.5	3.6	5.7	5.8	7.9	8.0	10.1	10.2	--	14.5-14.9
15.0-15.4	--	3.7	3.8	5.9	6.0	8.2	8.3	10.4	10.5	--	15.0-15.4
15.5-15.9	--	3.8	3.9	6.1	6.2	8.4	8.5	10.8	10.9	--	15.5-15.9
16.0-UP	--	3.9	4.0	6.3	6.4	8.7	8.8	11.1	11.2	--	16.0-UP

STANDARDIZATION

A sample of 100 residents was randomly drawn from the population of 463 residents at Lakeland Village. The sample drawn was examined with respect to distribution by sex, age, adaptive behavior classification, and measured intelligence classification. These distributions are presented in Table 3.

Table 3

DESCRIPTIVE STATISTICS OF STANDARDIZATION SAMPLE

Size of Pop. Sampled		Sample Size		Distribution by Sex	
Census	463	N	100	Male 53%	Female 47%

Distribution by Age		Distribution by Adaptive Behavior Class		Distribution by Measured Intell. Class	
Mean	31.4	Mild	9%	Mild	12%
Minimum	12.8	Moderate	9%	Moderate	5%
Maximum	74.9	Severe	24%	Severe	36%
Range	62.1	Profound	53%	Profound	44%
Stnd. Dev.	12.2	Other	5%	Other	3%

Grid scores, Vineland Social Maturity Scale Scores (SA's), and intelligence test scores (MA's and IQ's) were collected for each of the 100 residents in the sample. Depending upon the level of retardation and age, the following intelligence tests were employed: Kuhlmann Revision of the Binet-Simon Examination, Stanford-Binet Intelligence Scale, Merrill-Palmer Scale of Mental Tests, Slosson Intelligence Test, Bayley Scales of Infant Development, and Wechsler Adult Intelligence Scale. Wechsler IQ scores were converted to MA's by using the formula $MA = IQ \times CA/100$. The highest CA employed for substitution was 16. The distribution of the Grid, SA, MA and IQ scores are presented in Table 4.

Table 4

GRID SCORE, SA, AND MA/IQ DISTRIBUTIONS*

Grid Scores	Mean	Minimum	Maximum	Range	Std. Err.	Std. Dev.
Eating	5.09	0.45	12.80	12.35	0.30	2.98
Toileting	5.59	0.15	16.00	15.85	0.38	3.82
Dressing	5.92	0.15	14.40	14.25	0.39	3.87
Health & Grooming	4.81	0.30	13.60	13.30	0.35	3.53
Communication	2.99	0.10	13.80	13.70	0.27	2.69
Mobility & Dexterity	4.80	0.20	14.40	14.20	0.36	3.55
Vocation & Recreation	3.71	0.20	15.20	15.00	0.32	3.16
Socialization	3.91	0.20	15.20	15.00	0.36	3.58
Orientation	3.06	0.10	13.80	13.70	0.27	2.67
Self-Direction	3.87	0.10	14.40	14.30	0.31	3.12
Average Dev. Level	4.37	0.40	12.80	12.40	0.31	3.04

SA and MA/IQ Scores	Mean	Minimum	Maximum	Range	Std. Err.	Std. Dev.
Social Age Scores	5.18	0.94	13.80	12.86	0.31	3.08
Mental Age Scores	4.42	0.45	12.80	12.35	0.28	2.76
IQ Scores	25.31	2.00	81.00	79.00	1.84	18.27

*All scores except for IQ scores are in years

Reliability

Two reliability studies were conducted using data collected for the sample of 100 residents. For the first study, content area consistency was determined by conducting correlations between skill cluster scores and by correlating the skill cluster scores with the full scale scores (ADL's). For the second study, test-retest reliabilities were determined by correlating the ADL's for two Grid's conducted for each resident in the sample. The intervals between test and retest were approximately one year. The results of the first study are presented in Table 5. The test-retest correlation for the second study is 0.9598. All correlations are significant at the .001 level of confidence.

Table 5

GRID WITHIN-TEST CORRELATIONS (Pearson r)*

Grid AREA	EAT	TOI	DRE	H&G	COM	M&D	V&R	SOC	ORI	S-D	ADL
EAT	---	.9245	.9368	.9489	.7712	.7705	.8544	.7978	.8210	.8490	.9393
TOI		---	.9399	.9569	.8081	.7914	.8771	.8297	.8375	.8843	.9610
DRE			---	.9570	.7725	.8016	.8400	.7920	.8134	.8710	.9467
H&G				---	.8042	.8204	.8654	.8241	.8321	.8711	.9619
COM					---	.6897	.8736	.8340	.9024	.7898	.8857
M&D						---	.8141	.8104	.6984	.7041	.8583
V&R							---	.9117	.9041	.8067	.9440
SOC								---	.8755	.8278	.9178
ORI									---	.8416	.9156
S-D										---	.9114
ADL											---

*All correlations are significant at the .001 level of confidence

Validity

Two concurrent validity studies were conducted comparing test data collected for the sample of 100 residents. For the first study, Grid scores were correlated with Vineland Social Maturity Scale scores (SA's). For the second study, Grid scores were correlated with the MA and IQ scores from intelligence tests. All of the tests correlated for an individual resident were part of a single testing battery, usually administered within a two week period. The results of the two validity studies are presented in Table 6. All correlations are significant at the .001 level of confidence.

Another concurrent validity study was conducted comparing two classification methods for the sample of 100 residents. In this study, each subject in the sample was classified for adaptive behavior using Grid ADL's applied in the classification procedure described in the preceding section, INTERPRETING AND USING THE RESULTS. These classifications were then compared to existing classifications that had been generated as part of the routine annual evaluations following existing AAMD guidelines. The psychologists doing the routine classifying were not aware that a correlational study would later be conducted using the classification data. Correlation of the adaptive behavior classification codes for the two sets of data yielded a Pearson correlation coefficient of 0.9575. This correlation is significant at the .001 level of confidence and represents an agreement of classification in 92% of the one hundred cases sampled.

Table 6

GRID SCORE CORRELATIONS (Pearson r) WITH SA AND MA/IQ SCORES*

Skill Cluster	Correlation With Social Age	Correlation With Mental Age	Correlation With IQ
Eating	0.8980	0.7977	0.8088
Toileting	0.8737	0.7779	0.8190
Dressing	0.8976	0.7854	0.7962
Health & Grooming	0.8981	0.7890	0.8121
Communication	0.8433	0.7998	0.8020
Mobility & Dexterity	0.7964	0.6560	0.7135
Vocation & Recreation	0.8729	0.7815	0.8227
Socialization	0.8337	0.7455	0.7835
Orientation	0.8681	0.8181	0.8238
Self-Direction	0.8240	0.7129	0.7442
Average Developmental Level	0.9307	0.8280	0.8566

*All correlations are significant at the .001 level of confidence

REFERENCES

Alpern, G. D. & Boll, T. J. **Developmental Profile.** Indianapolis: Psychological Development Publications, 1972.

Bayley, N. **Bayley Scales of Infant Development.** New York: The Psychological Corporation, 1969.

Caplan, F. **The First Twelve Months of Life.** New York: Bantam Books, Inc., 1980.

Caplan, F. & Caplan, T. **The Second Twelve Months of Life.** New York: Bantam Books, Inc., 1980.

Cone, J. D. & Hawkins, R. P. **Behavioral Assessment: New Directions in Clinical Psychology.** New York: Brunner-Mazel, 1976.

Doll, E. A. **Measurement of Social Competence: a Manual for the Vineland Social Maturity Scale.** Circle Pines: American Guidance Service, Inc., 1953.

Dunn, L. M. **Peabody Picture Vocabulary Test.** Circle Pines: American Guidance Service, Inc., 1965.

Frankenburg, W. K. & Dodds, J. B. The Denver Developmental Screening Test. **Journal of Pediatrics,** 1967, 71, 181-191.

Gesell, A. & Ilg, F. L. **Infant and Child in the Culture of Today.** New York: Harper & Row, 1943.

Gesell, A. & Ilg, F. L. **The Child from Five to Ten.** New York: Harper & Brothers Publishers, 1946.

Gessell, A., Ilg, F. L., & Ames, L. B. **Youth: the Years from Ten to Sixteen.** New York: Harper & Brothers, 1956.

Grossman, H. J. (Editor). **Manual on Terminology and Classification in Mental Retardation.** Washington, D.C.: American Association on Mental Deficiency, 1973.

Grossman, H. J. (Editor). **Manual on Terminology and Classification in Mental Retardation.** Washington, D.C.: American Association on Mental Deficiency, 1977.

Grossman, H. J. (Editor). **Classification in Mental Retardation.** Washington, D.C.: American Association on Mental Deficiency, 1983.

Heber, R. A manual on terminology and classification in mental retardation. **American Journal of Mental Deficiency,** 1961 (Monograph Supplement).

Hutton, W. O. & Talkington, L. W. **The Developmental Record.** Corvallis: Continuing Education Publications, 1974.

Ilg, F. L. & Ames, L. B. **Child Behavior.** New York: Barnes & Noble Books, 1972.

Ilg, F. L. & Ames, L. B. **School Readiness: Behavior Tests Used at the Gesell Institute.** New York: Harper & Row, 1972.

Jastak, J. F., Bijou, S. W. & Jastak, S. R. **Wide Range Achievement Test.** Delaware: Guidance Associates of Delaware, Inc., 1976.

Koontz, C. W. **Koontz Child Developmental Program: Training Activities for the First 48 Months.** Los Angeles: Western Psychological Services, 1974.

Nihira, K., Foster, R., Shellhaas, M., & Leland, H. **AAMD Adaptive Behavior Scale.** Washington, D.C.: American Association on Mental Deficiency, 1969.

Pulaski, M. A. S. **Understanding Piaget.** New York: Harper & Row, 1980.

Santa Cruz County Office of Education. **Behavioral Characteristics Progression Charts.** Palo Alto: VORT Corporation, 1973.

Staff (Community/Regional Services, Inc.). **Nebraska Client Progress System.** Lincoln: Community/Regional Services, Inc., 1973.

State of Washington (Inter-Institutional Assessment and Training Scales Committee, S. A. Belcher, Chairman). **Washington Assessment and Training Scales (WATS).** Olympia: Office of Research, 1969.

Stutsman, R. **Guide for Administering the Merrill-Palmer Scale of Mental Tests.** New York: Harcourt, Brace & World, Inc. 1948.

Terman, L. M. & Merrill, M. A. **The Stanford-Binet Intelligence Scale.** Boston: Houghton Mifflin, 1973.

Wechsler, D. **The Measurement and Appraisal of Adult Intelligence.** Baltimore: The Williams & Wilkins Company, 1958.

LV — Lakeland Village Adaptive Behavior

GRID

REPORT FORM

AVERAGE DEVELOPMENTAL LEVEL ☐

	03 MO	06 MO	12 MO	18 MO	02 YR	03 YR	04 YR	05 YR.	08 YR.	12 YR.	16 YR.	LEVEL
1. EATING	a b c d e	a b c d e	a b c d e	a b c d e	a b c d e	a b c d e	a b c d e	a b c d e	a b c d e	a b c d e	a b c d e	1.
2. TOILETING	a b c d e	a b c d e	a b c d e	a b c d e	a b c d e	a b c d e	a b c d e	a b c d e	a b c d e	a b c d e	a b c d e	2.
3. DRESSING	a b c d e	a b c d e	a b c d e	a b c d e	a b c d e	a b c d e	a b c d e	a b c d e	a b c d e	a b c d e	a b c d e	3.
4. HEALTH & GROOMING	a b c d e	a b c d e	a b c d e	a b c d e	a b c d e	a b c d e	a b c d e	a b c d e	a b c d e	a b c d e	a b c d e	4.
5. COMMUNI-CATION	a b c d e	a b c d e	a b c d e	a b c d e	a b c d e	a b c d e	a b c d e	a b c d e	a b c d e	a b c d e	a b c d e	5.
6. MOBILITY & DEXTERITY	a b c d e	a b c d e	a b c d e	a b c d e	a b c d e	a b c d e	a b c d e	a b c d e	a b c d e	a b c d e	a b c d e	6.
7. VOCATION & RECREATION	a b c d e	a b c d e	a b c d e	a b c d e	a b c d e	a b c d e	a b c d e	a b c d e	a b c d e	a b c d e	a b c d e	7.
8. SOCIALI-ZATION	a b c d e	a b c d e	a b c d e	a b c d e	a b c d e	a b c d e	a b c d e	a b c d e	a b c d e	a b c d e	a b c d e	8.
9. ORIENTATION	a b c d e	a b c d e	a b c d e	a b c d e	a b c d e	a b c d e	a b c d e	a b c d e	a b c d e	a b c d e	a b c d e	9.
10. SELF DIRECTION	a b c d e	a b c d e	a b c d e	a b c d e	a b c d e	a b c d e	a b c d e	a b c d e	a b c d e	a b c d e	a b c d e	10.

NAME: _____ AGE: _____ DATE: _____

COMMENTS: _____

www.ingramcontent.com/pod-product-compliance
Lightning Source LLC
Chambersburg PA
CBHW081417270326
41931CB00015B/3305